AN UNEVEN BALANCE:

COLLECTED POEMS

BY

WALTER E. SMITH

ZD Publishing
Manufactured by Printing by Design
http://www.pbdink.com

An Uneven Balance

Copyright @ 2013 by Walter E. Smith

All rights reserved under International and Pan-American copyright conventions. No part of this book may be reproduced, stored in a retrieval system or transmitted in any form, electronic, mechanical or by other means, without written permission of the author.

ISBN: 978-1-4675-8967-3

Library of Congress

Cataloging in Publication Data

OTHER WORKS BY THE SAME AUTHOR

Bibliographies

Joseph Conrad: A Bibliographical Catalogue of His Major First Editions.

Charles Dickens in the Original Cloth: A Bibliographical Catalogue of the First Appearance of His Writings in Book Form in England. 2 vols.

The Bronte Sisters: A Bibliographical Catalogue of First and Early Editions, 1846-1860.

Elizabeth C. Gaskell: A Bibliographical Catalogue of First and Early Editions, 1848-1866.

Anthony Trollope: A Bibliography of His First American Editions. A Supplement to Michael Sadleir's TROLLOPE: A BIBLIOGRAPHY.

Charles Dickens: A Bibliography of His First American Editions, 1836-1870. The Novels with SKETCHES by BOZ.

Poetry

A Flash of Ohs

A Quiet Place and Other Poems

Contents

With Icy Glow	1
We Think of Life	2
A Death in the House	3
Pittsburgh Landing Again	4
Past Thoughts	5
A Dress for Thanksgiving	6
To Create a Poem	7
Still Life	8
Waiting in a Terminal	9
Near Another Change	10
A Visit	11
Old Age	12
Signs and Symbols	13
Do You Know Me?	14
Surrounded by Snow	15
Often When Time	16
The Final Visit	17
A Garden Visit	18
Parts	19
A Return	20
A Period Out of Self	21
Children Playing in Sand	22
The Oak at 5th and A, N.E.	23
The End of Fear	24
A Spot a Cal State	25
The Slimy Thing	26
I Enjoy My Garden	27
Spring Is an Active Elf	28
Recycled Days	29
Tired	30
A Balance Lives	31
If I Could Stay Away	32
Bygone Deaths	33
A Plea of Sadness	34
Fall	35
Guess Who?	36

Who Am I?	37
Epigram	38
The Eternal Sea	39
Today	40
The Sun	41
How Crisp the Autumn Season	42
Work	43
I Sat Alone	44
Physics and Semantics	45
Learning	46
Camelot	47
Progress	48
Movements	49
I Laid My Uniform to Rest	50
The Doctor's Office	51
No Return	52
Physics	53
How Clear the Sun	54
My Time Has Lingered	55
Lost Time	56
A Glove	57
Glimpses of a Library	58
Memories	59
A Watchman	60
Semantics	61
A Sermon	62
Pictures	63
I See a Man	64
Thoughts	65
An Offer	66
Paradise Enow	67
Unnamed Graveyards	68
Au Bon Pain	69
The Woods	70
When Death First Came	71
The Power of Words	72
The Tall Soldier	73
I've Seen the Angels Gather Round	74
Stamps	75
A Creative Form	76
A Form of Drama	77

Here is Enough	78
Education	79
A Visit Below	80
A Place Inbetween	81
A Brief Reflection	82
Welcome Now the Morning Spring	84
A Body Dresses Flesh and Heat	85
Times Away	86
Death Is Like a Hungry Axe	87
Death	88
A Naught at Times	89
Reflections in a Mall	90
The Heart Rejects	91
My Soul Petitions	92
Another Day in Milk and Honey	93
A Woman in Union Station	94
Stages	95
Our Daily Bread	96
The Delicate Balance	97
Extrapolations	98
Perfect Unions	99
A Wander	100
Aristotelian Acorns in Reverse	101
A Search for Heaven	102
A Summary of Life	103
Dark Days	104
A Taste of Time	105
A Hole in the Fence on Albany Avenue	106
An Old Myth	107
The Early Sun	108
Whence the Coming?	109
The Spirit's Prison	110
I Tried My Hand	111
It Isn't Fair to Die	112
Some Sins	113
A Spider Plots His Matrix	114
How Blessed I Trudge	115
A Facet of Water	116
The Ashes Grew	117
Sometimes In a Quiet Pause	118
Shadows	119

A Dot with Wire Legs	120
Life Is a Constant Drama	121
The March Begins with Human Joy	122
Old Time's a Patent Devil	123
Holidays	124
Silent Seeds	125
The Lightning Streaks	126
If Quiet Homes	127
The Massive Rocks	128
What Choice Had I	129
My Life Begins Each Waking Day	130
A Little Late	131
How Little Life Expends	132
The Sun No Longer Sets Reward	133
Another Spring	134
All Children Battle Healthy Sleep	135
One Creature in Nature	136
A Mattress of Gossip	137
Update on an Urn	138
She Came with Welcome Sound	139
Nature's Atoms	140
Life Is an Interlude	141
O To Be Alive	142
The Sun's an Old Physician	143
Old Age Again	144
When Mirrors Move	145
Emotions' Well	146
Race with Time	147
She Left Us	148
Certain Moods	149
No Fault with Crows	150
A Fearful Doubt	151
The Living Can't Abide	152
Commentary with Poem	153
Alone in Time	155
Joy to Be Alive	156
Splendor	157
The Essence Lies	158
Die in Pieces	159
Matter of Waiting	160
A Hallway	161

On Keats	162
Graduation in Nipomo	163
Research	164
Contrast	165
Acute Angles	166
A Barker	167
Midnight Chow	168
Lines	169
History	170
CSULB: 50 Years Today	171
Changes	173
Violinist on the Subway	174
A Butterfly	175
When Wolves Turn White Once More	176
Homeless	177
Growing Shadows	178
To Hide a Thought	179
Mindless Things	180
Fast Food Outside	181
After Shot	182
Except in Thought	183
The Onyx Floor	184
The Eyes Take Pictures	185
Return to Change	186
Dylan	187
The Del	188
There's No Evidence	189
The March of Time	190
Of All the Times	191
Pro Life	192
After a Rain	193
Rain	194
Bumblebees	195
At the Movies	196
The Honeybees	197
Return	198
Warblers	199
All We Know	200
If Perchance a Lustful Want	201
A Short History Lesson	202
Valerie	203

With Icy Glow

With icy glow the children stare
   At gowns and sundry ware;
The mannequins stand inches away
   Unmoved in suave display.

The poppies live in distant view
   Among the scrubby oaks;
A farmer hears the passing train
   And feels its rich allure.

A thought can often hypnotize
   And yield a hopeful rest;
How close we live to nearby death
   Each merging breath reflects.

We Think of Life

We think of life in terms of time
And label daily parts,
Routine and varied habits marked
Italicized at starts.

Calendars denote the years
And months indent to weeks;
A watch condenses math again
And measures things unique.

Such physics other creatures lack,
Their nerves not finely wrought.
But nature creates many forms
Perhaps above our thought.

Some concepts transfer words to space
And matter factors climb,
Physicians swear a heart unmoved
Rescinds a person's time.

A Death in the House

The second day after death a strange
Quiet locks the house and unnoticed things
Loom large as seconds swell slowly
In the ticking air and whispers sear across
Old coats of furniture wax like running fires.

A streak of morning sun burns through a slit
In the drapes and lights the stale ashes clinging
To the grate, then moves to polish wear on stairs.
In the kitchen dishes chatter above muffled
Voices that endeavor to seal sound from the dead.

In the parlor men impatient fumble with their watches
And sit hidden in chairs behind their tapping feet.
The children unsure of the occasion or their participation wait
In stiff clothes for family guidance and stare
About wondering if normalcy will ever return.

And the busy women bustling with sorrow too hurried
To think collapse into silent sobs
When pauses occur and wipe their hearts with aprons
Of love, then begin anew to erase the drawers
And open forever the eyes of yesterday's memories.

A procession of black follows behind Latin
Words, and wizened mourners shrink a syllable.

Pittsburgh Landing Again

Deeper in winter than summer's sun,
Past the exuberant hope of spring,
Calm to the colors of falling leaves,
The soldiers rest in straight parade.

Graveyard by record with foreign names,
Further attachment is ordered file;
None can decipher the chiseled marks
Now merged again by weather's hand

Into the rows of marble altars
That stand amid the seamless grass.
Only God discerns their faces
And hears their vows of endless creed.

Past Thoughts

We little thought those days would fade
Like misty morning air,
And time would shrink from lasting light
To narrow slits of prayer.

How quick the moss enshrouds the rocks
As shadows move the sun;
The sweat on brows no longer grows
As detours block our run.

But children step inside our walk
And tread atop our wear,
And waken visions loud with life
That beckon past despair.

Their racing joy exhumes our blood,
Their actions swell our veins,
Forgotten truths revive again
From countless hidden gains.

Some secret things the mind enfolds
And stores for future need,
When bones request a soothing salve
Or morning wants a seed.

A Dress for Thanksgiving

The younger woman slid the closet door
Aside and waited while her friend focused
Her pasty eyes on gaudy garments, limp
And dated, that sagged on wire hangers, alone
And eerie, like headless forms of crucified ghosts.

The cotton candy hair and alabaster neck
Protruded from sweater and blankets on the wheelchair
Where, captive and warm, like a freshly dressed fowl,
She stretched the marble column that buttressed her head
In a fierce effort to discern her remaining choices.

Transmission slow as each dress creaked apart
On the pipe rack; she selected, demurred, turned
Away her wattled chin, and the incident passed
Unresolved as another concern roused her thoughts.
The younger woman sought her spidery hand.

To Create a Poem

My careless mind often strives
To convey a moving thought into
Expressive words via a compact poem,
But struggles with meter and metaphor
Produce lines that invariably distort
My original concept, while connecting accidentals
Rub awkwardly against substantives
And result in undue stress and cacophony
That further disrupt the flow of rhythm.
Wayward images intrude upon
The process and distraction and lax concentration
Further diminish the creative effort.
The final product, even a skillful
Transmission, is a glimmer of the inner truth.

Still Life

A cleaning after death unearths old photo
Albums long ignored in bottom drawers
Or locked in treasured chests consigned to attics.

The pages crackle as they're turned from dried glue
And cellophane tape, now hard and yellow, used
To mount crudely the prints to the loose and soft
Black matte paper. Always neat

And poised in sacred stances and beaming with set
Smiles, the subjects centered on the camera's lens
And waited for the steady word and magic click
That gave their current images instant immortality.

Children with blond eyes squinted in the sun.
And the foolish grins of young girls later
Smoothed to haloed love as they appeared with babies.
The farmers stood awkward in Sunday clothes,
While old people forced more lines on their hurt faces.

Some pictures of unknown or forgotten relatives and friends,
Still merry and warm in captured time, were
Carefully extracted and only vestiges of paper
Tears marked the places where they had laid.

Waiting in a Terminal

High quick voices, sometimes others
With foreign intonations, jabbed half-intelligible
Announcements periodically to the unattentive crowd herded
Together for travel about the domed arena.
A woman old in brown stockings shuffled
To a seat, the ribbed flesh beneath her eyes
Rippled as she moved like concentric circles
Spawned by a pebble dropped in a morning pond.
I thought of Duke Ellington's melting countenance.
Another woman sat stiff and blank
Nearby, the lines in her face turned upward
And short white coils pinched her chin.
A youth massaged the thighs of his girlfriend.
Squatting on the carpet, a mother beat cereal
In a cup then spooned herself and a babe in stroller.
A middle-age woman, seated in a corner,
Sucked her thumb and clutched a teddy bear.
I shut my eyes and wondered if I had enough No.
2 pencils for my task at the Houghton Library.

Near Another Change

Her legs cycled beneath the sheets
Like a struggling fish wrapped in cloth;
Her head shook and she gargled words
About family truths and a hurt mind.
Each hour a race crossed her face.

Then overnight a calmness came:
The head shrunk and fell into the hair
And the skin smoothed and sat still.
The poised mouth awaited communion
And the body became comfortable to view.

Only her erratic breathing told
Of her leaving, and its frequency marked
Her path to eternity. A sound away
The family, unable to amend the solemn

Mystery, spoke of feeble things,
Paused to listen, and accepted the concern
Which no godless effort could cure.

A Visit

I visited the streets I knew,
Where as a boy I played,
The granite walks were now cement,
The houses strange and bent.

I asked about myself
To puzzled folk I saw,
They had no sense of me
Or friends who bided there.

My field was filled with stones,
The ground undressed and lumpy;
I turned and heard unseen
Sounds declare and then fade.

The place was foreign now to me
Bereft of former ties:
How quickly time corrupts the truth
And fills the mind with lies.

Old Age

As I totter near my waiting grave,
The whistling wind forks my bones
And time unmasks my melting flesh
In the slow growing darkness of space;
My mind yet supersedes such timely arguments
And pursues each day with measured hope,
Borne from spans of refuge and luster
And prolonged by heart-singing joys which echo
In my fading thoughts like a happy jinni
Who guides me through life's wonted routines.
As the complex equation of my being dims,
Equal and balanced cancellations occur
And the simple remaining symbol will serve
To mark and define the truth of my whole.

Signs and Symbols

No mark is left by time but other symbols
Stamped and figured in mind from senses read
And often thought again from further signs
And symbols born to bring alive the past.

Each movement loses force because all symbols
Dull with added ones, though most of those
Are ghosts revived. Our meaning struggle seeks
To sequence life in union lines of worth.

Some days in years remain from proof or linger
In cells dented by sparks. The rest are hidden
Elsewhere. Our final sign bequeaths a symbol
Even more abstract than current time.

Do You Know Me?

Your eyes invent an image first
And place its print with passion files.
Then talk and background enter sums
Which further alter concept's growth;
And contact often adds new lines
While time enhances colored tints.
Each noun creates another look
Which tunes the whole until all years
Abandon sight and merge in thought.
Your final impression unmasks all acts
And I often become the same.

Surrounded by Snow

Surrounded by snow in a giant's chair
And dressed in kingly Christmas robes
Santa transmitted sparks of joy
To me as I waited to ascend his throne.
I floated to his lap and listened to sweet
Whispers about wants
Flow from his furry beard before
A final hug and slide down his leg
Ended the visit with a thrilling gift.
The photos in those days were developed in our minds.
One memorable visit of twenty-five cents
Conveyed untold power to a boy:
A policeman's badge with whistle and club.

Each year as the line became longer
My visits moved farther back
And ended as I approached Santa's threshold.
From a distance I sometimes pause to watch
Santa and the happy flow of children;
But the rapture I knew has gone with the boy
And only a smile now flags in my heart.

Often When Time

Often when time is kept waiting
And our minds and eyes are coiled
To notice things unseen in the course
Of tethered routine do movements and dress
Reveal the traits and narratives of our being.

A man bent forward to his waist,
Like an attacking soldier or as if an ironing board
Were lodged in his back, presses across
The Venetian lobby to a beach-clothed woman
Who stands quietly in her mocking curves.

No business to ride, children dance
In their painted voices and bounce against
The rumps of their mothers which buffer their joy
Like cradles ready to receive them.

Some stickman move like hospital needles
Searching about for hidden life,
While other men with seals beneath
Their teeshirts juggle their hairless heads.

Such pictures unveil untold commentaries
That chase time into forgetful reality.

The Final Visit

He always stops to take a breath
And hold the blood in rest;
Then makes the mind an empty source,
The flesh a hardened shell.

What was he takes beyond our scope
Outside the frame of life,
And we in tears and rites of faith
Await his chancy stay.

A Garden Visit

When Frances visits her garden
Nature declares a holiday;
Spiders close their shops;
Ants parade their children about,
While crows align the balcony
And bend a novel eye.

Her tender smile warms new buds
And stretches them beyond their pods.
She looses shoes and tightens care
And alters awkward coats,
Then measures quick their circumstance
And gently grooms their etiquette.

She cleans away all breakfast trays,
And flowers toll in silent cheers
As slowly she ushers in the day.
In routine course she greets all plants,
Whose hearts erupt as she moves by,
And seeds of their love cling to her clothes.

Parts

We grow in molds after birth -
Alike with varied traits - beneath
The smile of pink and blue and social
Hints of space, time and event.
Sound is another fact to address
Our different selves: The farmer in the dell;
Cries from bullet-cracking bones;
The hum inside electronic caves;
A praying nomad pinching his whiskers.
Speech is the noise of our immortal
Longing for calmness of our souls.
Certain tasks and customs blend
Into a detailed form of unity
Which distance classes humanity.

A Return

It is good to be at Yale again
And visit the quiet stones, where friends
Remain in unwrinkled time and talk
Through the crack of a pigeon's wings in tones
That welcome my still and coming approach.
The weather blurs the chiseled letters
And slowly smoothes the granite facades.
New steps carve the marble floors
And shadows wake along the halls
As I pass and turn my thoughts around.
Old glossy prints preserve our youth,
Now stored in files for forgotten eyes.
One pale night I heard the howls
Of students swirl down Chapel Street.

A Period Out of Self

When travail surrenders time and clearness
Stills all thoughts, and movement pauses
Cells, a calmness halts all process
And union of emptiness binds in the whole.
The sun veils its burn, the winds
Run untouched, and sound loses
Voice in the nearness of spacial event.
Then one perceives the unknown and dwells
A fraction in single, unbroken happiness.

Children Playing in Sand

I watch them fill their metal pails with moist
Sand, wrenched with tin shovels from beneath
The beige furrows that glisten in the morning sun.
Once filled, they overturn the colored pails
And begin to pat shapes of castles, mounds,
Or imagined creatures which change with sculptured dabs
And grow with added casts until molded
To satisfaction to show for praise or paddled impulsively
By disappointment and abandoned for other sudden attractions.
Quickly the creations dwindle to linear levels
By the crush of trampling feet and the impartial wash
Of the ocean's calm and endlessly soothing hands.
Years ago I recall an old woman took
Sand from my box to clean on certain days.

The Oak at 5th and A, N.E.

Quiet rain washes the ribbed morocco
Bark black and settles crystal beads
Along its fingers that dangle above Federal
Houses and often weigh misguided crows.
Cameo gapes mark its shoulders maimed
By veteran time, and beaten curbstones crumble
Into melting silt that paddles erratically at its base
About the edges of a rolling rainbow stream.
Its torso rests on swollen padded paws
That imitate the feet of a William and Mary Chest;
Yards away gnarled roots appear,
Isolated and hard, like sudden bones from a growing
Grave; light from the Capitol's dome reflects
In its shadows. Later, it will change as the months move.

The End of Fear

The bubbles of fear erupt with increased frequency
As age extracts the confidence of youth and replaces
It with debilitating torment: doubts about luggage
In the overhead rack, alarming news items,
A burnt out bulb, the angle of a screw - all these
Blister the mind and linger until some concrete
Assurance dissipates the fear and purges its unreasonableness.
Any real or imagined alteration begins the fermentation
Which grows and dies constantly until one final
Growing unchange levels the oscillations into a breathless
Line. Now the silly unmovement occurs:
The playing hide and seek with a sleeping grandparent,
The accidental snap of a main computer switch.

A Spot at Cal State

There's a spot hidden from traffic and daily
Bustle unknown behind a barrier of shrubs
Where koi glide across a dark green
Pond in lines of color, while others calmly
Circle cattails with slow majestic rolls
Of their fins; some gather near clay banks
By children, who tease their puffing mouths for food.
Guarded by cement lions, few find this way
And move soundlessly along its pebbled walk
And across the bridges into soft light and trees.
Free from work, visitors sit on wolf-stone
Slabs and view activity in distant concepts.
Everything is balanced in this synagogue past time,
Where nature poses unabashed in breathless life.

The Slimy Thing

The slimy thing with lumpy nodes,
Whose peppered skin is slippery green,
Has global eyes unfit for his trunk
And bandaged feet so oddly obscene.

He favors bogs and stagnant pools
And sites that cool and cloud the day;
But summer nights when mosquitoes abound
And air exudes a sweating spray,

He swells a gland to remarkable size
Then exhales pulses of guttural sound
That bounce about my cabin walls
Like grotesque horns from a geese pound.

Neither flashlights nor friends, except
During hunts, can still this persistent boor,
Who resumes his call when quiet's restored
With greater conviction than ever before.

This bane of sleep vacation nights
The weary mind accepts with time,
But if a rival creature starts
The tumult breeds a compound crime.

I Enjoy My Garden

I enjoy my garden, such soothing therapy,
To sit amid the flowers and hear their symphony.
The sun lights the setting, tuning is by bees,
Nature is the maestro, his baton the morning breeze.

Time opens the shadows to wake the harmony,
Crows on arthritic feet line the balcony.
Hummers hover and constantly change their seats
Butterflies in tandem dizzily swim in heats.

In a crescendo of flaming color, the allegro starts:
Hollyhocks and foxgloves blast through their parts;
Roses and lavateras sound deftly the trill;
Violets waft the melody among the daffodils.

Grass forms a chorus for the song set,
Daisies and pansies dance the bright minuet.
Naked ladies add a scent of grace,
Hydrangea's percussion ends the fast pace.

Eternity in Eden could offer nothing more
Than the life I experience outside my kitchen door.

Spring Is an Active Elf

Spring is an active elf who stores
In time old winter's worth
And builds a cradle of growing life
To welcome summer's birth.

He starts his chores at equinox
By dusting clean the stars;
Then slowly sponges heavens cheeks
And tweaks the isobars.

He hangs the sun and clouds in place
And draws the croci pods,
And turns the swallows loose to find
Their homes among facades.

The robins hop in tandem then
Pause to check their place;
Lilacs start to shed perfume
Upon a poppy's face.

The daffodils and harlequins
He paints en plein air,
And signs of his whole plebiscite
Are legion everywhere.

Activities to calculate,
Impossible to despair,
Require special instruments
To pantomime the air.

Recycled Days

Life is a string of recycled days
That dangles by air to a run of blood
And swings about with regenerate words,
Evanescing by wear its rosary of flesh.

The daily sun reheats old thoughts
And washes former wishes away
Like drying waves on mitred shores,
While dreams coalesce with ripened growth.

How welcome the sound of distant bells
That echo the sway of hangers brushed
By busy people alive in closets
Who dare the confines of gnawing change.

Tired

Tired beyond any other feeling
Alone in a field with wise corbies,
The sun visits the quiet flesh
And grass shelters severed parts.

Free to move now at ease,
How small and empty the ground.
What pursuit was measured here
On those horrid three days?

The curtains have opened to clear smoke,
The stratosphere has caught the din,
Everything is less than it was,
Except for a number of chiseled stones.

It's hard to make something from nothing,
But pictures and words don't lie;
A true course cannot be set long,
The compass jitters and truth hides.

A Balance Lives

A balance lives among our griefs
In houses made of tears,
Where room of empty solitude
Have windows blanked by years.

On worn nights in hopeless press
When demons rend the mind,
It quickly gauges wayward trends
And slowly quells their force.

No steps can scope its coming,
No box conclude its start;
A factor of time in measured thoughts
Returns all symbols to zero.

If I Could Stay Away

If I could stay away all day
And wake the next today
Repeat each time unbroken years
That house the boarder life,
How sacred would existence be
To dwell outside my role?
To see another stable force
Becomes a balanced thought.

But when all nouns recoil in fear
And situations flee
The world of self regains control
And routs serenity.
Acceptance fosters peaceful change,
A scion of eternity.

Bygone Deaths

Our thoughts reflect on bygone deaths
And cast a light on time,
Reviving states in brighter hues
Than ever lived when prime.

The scent of pine at Christmas warms
The shadows grown on snow,
A pirouette in gingham turns
A smile into a glow.

And holy sins that words forgave
Extend like running cracks,
A fading face that wakened love
Unfolds now artifacts.

The children frail in coffins spill
Their ceaseless anarchy,
An awful leisure charts the course,
Majestic potpourri.

A Plea of Sadness

A plea of sadness hovers round
Like misty morning wakes
And wrinkles thoughts with heavy press
On sides that empty takes.

Its power covers rueful seeds
With claws of wet despair
And poisons ageless waterways,
Miasma sifts the air.

No voice can penetrate its realm,
No touch intrude its stay,
All functions halt in breathless hue
And time erases day.

Of curses none can match its mark
And leave such icy pain,
As bodies set in open graves
Rebuke their thirst for rain.

Fall

The sun awakens late in fall
And wears a tepid tone;
Its attitude infects the earth
And topples summer's throne.

The trees begin to show a rage
Then pause to pull their hair;
As apples leap and tumble round,
The grass refuses care.

The wind exhales an icy drink
And roses need a shave;
Coyotes mute their evensong
While bulbs secure a grave.

Winter peeks through coming days
And notes this turned priority
Then calculates the serenade
To bring about conformity.

Guess Who?

Between the flow and backward hiss
Our multicolored roles exist.
The morning feast and nightly rant,
The daily gossips over life,
The sift again when strangers meet,
The mix anew when lives unfold,
Hide ourselves in variant states
And create idols which blind truth.
The years abandon fact and symbols
Rule all thoughts until time
Unmasks all acts and dresses change.

Who Am I?

The self is like a moving tune
Played by time on a harp of life:
Each string's a role we pluck to show
To those about our holy nature.
Hearers judge the melody based
On form and text, with added bars
They interject to note their pride and taste.
Conclusion comes with muffled claps –
Each heard an altered song – until
The piece remains and self is one.

Epigram

Many longings haunt our years,
A human gamut of aching wants,
Which if fulfilled deprive the dreams
Of nature's stirring within our souls.
Varied ones linger in each
Mind which routine to another dissipates
Drive. A victor relishes less his
Prize than the wounded dying afield.

The Eternal Sea

The sea has steady work to do
Throughout each cycled day
And never stops to rest or view
Its progress under way.

At night its hushing song befits
The blanket sleep of night;
Its gentle booms in measured bits
Repel a fitful fright.

It sews a dress of tinsel thread
Along the naked sand
And waves its trowel across that bed
Of fresh cemented land.

It washes pebbles bright with sun
And offers them retail
Along the shore to anyone
Whose choice a form of sale.

My tickled feet when just a boy
Then sensed its graceful force;
Ambition grown and passing joy
Have fled its constant course.

Today

We have not time to stop or think,
Some trivia might escape.
We swell our minds with passing thoughts
And never reject their rape.

Our days are filled with cant and noise
No sacred truth or calm.
Electrons race about our rings
And threaten human balm.

Our business greed supplants our need
And riches make us free.
All lilacs bend to heavy sword
And yield to grasping bee.

Unworldly rights defame concrete,
No basic proof exists.
The pain some feel inside themselves
Despite discount persists.

Although our world rejoices night
And tramples foreign hope,
A few await with sharp insight
To cut our gibbet's rope.

The Sun

The sun arose like a lazy balloon
All orange in the distant whisper of air.
She covered stars with blankets of glow
Then stretches to a ring of spiked rays
That peeked through heaven's blinds to see
And warm the earth in solemn rapport.

The hills began to wash their faces
As brooks gargled to color their speech,
While trees absorbed the radiant fuel
And butterflies trickled in the tinsel spark.
Bees groomed and polished their pincers
Then swayed to kiss the lilac blooms.

Small wonder pagan soldiers raised
Their plumes to her in life-giving praise;
Workers today in stout fields
Pause in thought to anoint her blessings.

Then soft as a cat, her day's chores
Done, her nightgown on – no shameful
Pride to bequeath – she strolls home
Beyond the horizon and eases into bed.

How Crisp the Autumn Season

How crisp the autumn season comes
To dry the summer's reason;
How hard the winter holds in place
The cracking spring of birth.

The oceans march in step to moon
And slowly tramp the land;
The stars obey existing laws
And hide around their galaxy.

The day uncovers sleeping night
And welcomes home the sun;
Philosophy works the math of time
And figures the worth of matter.

Little I know about such things,
But sense the love of Frances,
Whose daily presence enters my world
And anchors my concept of heaven.

Work

Life is a matter of work performed
Incessantly by cells which explode silently
In constant regeneration and multiply within
Infinite weddings of disparate births.

When running seeds unhook empty
Eggs the process begins anew.
Cells within cells labor with might
Until they breach to enter the world.

Alone in a species of being the internal
Skeleton fights the plagues of nature
And moves unseen by time to create
A focus and a measure of six-sided reality.

Who dares demean the order of ants
Or seeks the whale's symbolic role?
No secrets sought can be revealed
Beyond the circle which seals the cells.

I heard a breathing sound by me
Which mimicked still by formless sleep.
Rest is but pivotal work
As cells align for a chemical change.

I Sat Alone

I sat alone inside my sins
And never purged their source
Until with time a human growth
Of reason freed myself.

I placed a chain of foreign force
With links upon my thoughts
Which held in place a constant goal
Divorced from sacred nature.

The rusted tie now dangles loose,
A thing to sometimes ponder,
While traces of its former might
Still whitens my behavior.

Physics and Semantics

My dancing feet in a mirror glide
Like sliding paws on a sheet of ice
Untouched by human pulls which wear
The shoes in real and measured time.

My hands conduct and wrinkle air
In sweeping clefs which gnaw the bones
Of fingered growth and time again
Reveals slowly their inside routes.

Mirages glow in raining thoughts
Across the pavement of mind and wave
Before my eyes a sequence past
Of truths in lines of quiet song.

My pulsating rings are a living wonder
Which will fade and change events until
Death unravels my sign and I
Become a concept in my other selves.

Learning

If I could while my time away
In never-ending books
And read all things which ever were
I'd dwell in Eden's niche.

With Ursa's leash around my hand
I'd walk the sky and grade
The moon with sparkled night and seek
A hidden star. I'd set the sun

Below my feet and test the earth's
Delight then peek inside an eagle's
Eye and grasp the being ring.
On other days I'd turn a page

And watch all pirates flee, or take
The cold from mountain tops and warm
The fruitful sea. I'd trudge through life
Forevermore with Atlas on my back.

Camelot

I do not hear the forest talk in tones
Of green delight, nor do I see misty
Morning coil above a sanguine pond.
As guiltless birth erupts, the foxglove ties
Its tolling tongue, the lilac holds its breath.
Men in tiger money roam along
A pathless course, gobbling air with rhythmic
Noise, while women hide in male array
As children rattle Popeye's grave and steal
The swords from clocks to vie and quest for fame.
All toys have lost their turn and tasteless wine
And wafers only cloud my soul. I dwell
Unfit in Ares' clothes, a boneless skeleton
Dangling by thought and hope in vacant time.

Progress

A roman candle streaks through the night
In wayward course and dares the dark
With frenzied mission until it bursts
At terminal point than shocks the air
With a shower of sizzles which fall and fade
And merge at last in quiet blindness.

The simple turn of a knob alters
A balanced sinewave into a jagged sawtooth
Shape, while another attenuates it into a ripple.
A final twist filters it into a line.
All is silent like deleting email.

However, new suns always erupt
To scatter old shadows and to burn with undying
Propellant which fits all things above
The boundaries of heaven and never ceases
To lighten the nature of action and thought.

Movements

How quickly time has taken my summer years
And pushed their glow into roaming shadows,
Where only pieces remain to scar my thoughts
As my x-ray self wanders in the pluperfect.

How quickly stars retain their smiles and never
Upset the milky way always turning
Like mannequins in department store window displays,
Silent in ancient talk to my plastered ears.

How fiercely oceans plow the crusty land
And overturn concrete creeds, whose barren
Weeds fail to nourish starving mankind,
Then plant and water seeds for another heaven.

I Laid My Uniform to Rest

I laid my uniform to rest among
The ciphered days where its pitted brass
And sticky cloth shone unabashed again
In crowded parades and symbolic rites
Which dressed so neat its clean gabardine.

It was after the time I ate with faceless men,
Who hid in open graves amid the clamor
And burning sweat of metal, then rose to begin
Battle over barren land and only succeeded
In bandaging the bloody ground with their whitened bodies.

It was in the time when confetti flowed like happy snow
And smiles kissed the air and my green bed
Offered safe repose in healthy sounds
Which erupted in the kitchen to prove and echo the stirring
Love my joyful return welcomed home.

It was a new time when poppies colored and songs
Of mocking birds sliced the silent air
And bees bent blossoms on the lavatera trees
And the grass stretched across the sacred earth
To cover and smooth away my fading memories.

The Doctor's Office

Some heavy women with puffy–lined faces
Sit in slacks among the hanging minutes.
One stares about sucking her teeth fiercely,
Then stops to search a bulging basket at her feet.
Another chews her teeth and splashes through pages
Of a photo magazine, her eyes flashing across
The corners of each page without pause.
The thighs of another are so thick that her knees
Cannot touch yet she holds a black-leathered Bible
In her lap which she reads silently, her head down,
Slowly pointing out each word with her left
Index finger while moving her painted lips.
A tall thin man, whose skin is as white
As his hair, leans back in his chair, his knees
Reach above his waist, his legs not unlike
Those of men freed from holocaust camps.
A foreign family hides in a still corner
Until the children's impatience erupts in a noisy
Fight which is quickly quelled by their mother's eyes.
New patients race though required forms,
Pausing only to ponder their medical history
And fumbling their purses for insurance cards and details.
Much is signed illegibly, often without comprehension,
Trusting to the skill of the administering physician, before
Racing back to the reception's windows then nervously
Turning to sit and wait in the selection process.
Suddenly a name is called and a patient arises.
The waiting and lost time cease and are forgotten.

No Return

If I returned to childhood,
To days the mind could not store,
Would current time connect
Old actions loose in thought?

The separate acts of parents,
The clouded bubbles in my nerves,
All burn for resolution
To see the makeup era.

But I would not be as I was then:
People would not know me or themselves;
I would not see them as they were;
Even pain could not show the truth.

Neither thought nor time
Have space for truthful reality.
Former sparks remain with me.
Gloomy shadows hide their ashes.

Physics

I packed a lunch the other day
And started for the sun.
I hop-scotched over continents
And splashed the seas for fun.
The planets served as stepping stones
Along the milky way,
The moon flashed its ashen light
And Venus smiled my way.
But then some dreadful roars
Cracked the empty air.
They pushed against heaven's doors
And frightened angels there.
Arms of flame greeted me –
Such welcome turned me back –
I slid down through the galaxy
And dropped my toasted snack.

I'll keep my friend at distant times
And visit him away –
Enough to have him tender life
And calculate each day.

How Clear the Sun

How clear the sun uncovers fields
And dresses them in green
Then waters streams with silver lines
And washes shadows clean.

Butterflies attack the air
And bees besiege a rose;
Trees align their infantry,
The crows retain their pose.

How calm the action draws the scene
So still in distant thought,
The ideal time in captured dream
Until the real is sought.

My Time Has Lingered

My time has lingered past the words which said
    I shouldn't be, yet still the will and cap–
    Sules keep the daily cells in tune; ahead
    Acceptance beckons me with final wrap
    Of peace, but babies in the kitchen, noise
    In empty rooms deflect the normal term,
And thoughts of rites and running hope and joys
Which marked all seasons kiss the heart confirm
    The soul sustain the work of nature's rings.
Though knowledge slips and action wanes and health
    Tiptoes away, I battle gloom with springs
Of love which line my face with wizened wealth.
    Each day domestic chores reclock the psalm
    Of life and trade its spoils for gathered calm.

Lost Time

How quickly turns another year
Whose numbers mark a total birth
Though most the digits ciphers yield,
A sequence still with minus sums.

Calendars map symbolic time
Whose routes continue sheet to sheet
By spatial tears and running ink
But never print a course return.

Our watches show romantic race
Though women straighten hope in place
And store their days for things renewed;
But striving men rejoice in calm,
Erase their lives with bare routine.

A Glove

My time unrolls like fingers from a glove
Which guards me from nature's bite in flower
Beds bright with roses and perfumed lilacs
And soft pansies that flag about throaty
Irises that loom alone in my youthful garden.
With little effort I remove the soiled
And soggy glove and hang it over a nail,
Where it dries and awaits use again whenever
I desire to venture into the joy of being
And work among the blooming beauty of spring.
How clean and clear my hand remains,
Protected by choice of this facile means.

Glimpses of a Library

The library rests like a tired relic
Buried beneath taller buildings where
Crowds of people with leather cases
Parade about in commercial clothes,
Too busy with business to consider its presence.

Over- pressurized security guards, bent by
Dull and empty time, who protect
This prison of learning, find solace
With their jobs in gossip with passing clerks
And by monitoring clocks until break periods.

Most who enter shuffle through the floors
In slovenly wear like houseless persons
Who seek interludes inside just to sit
And visit washrooms and perhaps read
And worship moments of untethered rest.

And children, forced to be there,
Accomplish their tasks with raging speed
Then flee to resume their easy fun.
Older others researching items
Work refreshed outside themselves.

Various sites in the rotunda hold
Blackened bronze plaques, some with engraved
Images, which celebrate unknown names
And dates of former librarians and benefactors
For their commendable services and civic honors.

A light rain in the courtyard outside
Tickles the young leaves of a maple
Tree, and makes them bounce in tacit delight.
The sudden return of people and noise
Awakens fret and levels all thought.

Memories

Outside quick thoughts in boxes bent
Recline the symbols of deeds and rites
That once rang in uncommon acts
And now gauge the concord of being.

Pecan flowers flake like burnt
Paper beside pitted bronze
Medals that rest blow sticky
Ribbons and pieces of disintegrating silk.
Whispers of advice are heard still
From curled photographs with ancient faces,
While sepias of forgotten or unknown persons
Are segregated – too sacred to discard – in hope
That someday their marks will be revived.
The most touching views are of children,
Who have long marched out of their pictures.

Such things are the fingers of a concerto of life
Which play across constructed time
Melodies that tune and calibrate the soul.

A Watchman

A spider works the graveyard shift
To guard my house from pesky things
When my watch ends in healthy sleep.
His territory's narrow – a cubbyhole
Or slot – marked with matrix threads
In which he stands a soldier still
Until a sharp invader tugs
Against his silky thoroughfare;
With thunder speed he cracks the foe
Noiselessly with swords of Swiss precision
That spin and quickly seal a strife.
Protector to hangman bundled in one
Escheats to stone from deeds done.
His battle scars are left behind
When sun uncovers his hidden bed.
No hired keeper can stay the worth
Of this transient who never seeks pay.

Semantics

If I could cancel open space
And cross erase zero time
And blank events that sanction me,
Then signs and symbols would converge
And sprout new rungs on ladder's being
And I would merge as one with God.

A Sermon

The rain delivered a sermon last night
More stirring and frank than Sunday's best,
For words alone cannot impart
The need to respect Nature's might.

His thunderous voice streaked and cracked,
Which woke the sky and household beds;
His arms flung across our roofs
And shingles jumped in rhythmic barrage.
Spears raced about in windy chants
And crashed against our helpless walls;
Pages ripped across our thoughts
And beating lines presaged horror;
His constant fury seemed to want
To reach inside and grasp our souls
And lock our lives in stony fear.
Suddenly in a flash of stark retreat
He fled to threaten another town.

All people praised the morning light
And felt the calm sun gently
Retrieve the damp and scattered excerpts.

Pictures

I watch the snowflakes whirl about
Like pesky flies upon the beach
Until they find a welcome site
And merge as one in docile heaps.

Then lilies yawn and tulips stretch
As the yellow sun bestirs the bees.
And girls with dolls move in years
While boys in blue rejoice and search.

Horses blend with shiny cars
And hills of green display their wares.
Parents carry shopping bags
Then stop to rest in the tired air.

The ground begins to hibernate; leaves
Untie themselves as winds erupt
With surly words; rain washes
Gloom from the street, and pumpkins smile.

Behind my window safe inside
Pictures live in cycled prints
Seen in sequence like calendar dates,
Unchanging nature eyes renewed.

I See a Man

I see a man standing in the sun
With his shadow walking behind him.
The repeated sequence decreases in height
Until it becomes a straight line.

I see a missile frozen in flight
With fuel exploding from its booster stage
Which creates mirages of dashed traces
Along its initial flight path.

I see young women in jeans, unable
To rise and continue themselves, sit
And talk about their brothers and laugh
And look to others and things for distraction.

I see the face of a tall case
Clock with its hand stopped at twelve,
Yet I hear its pendulum mark the moving
Seconds and toll the proper bells.

Sometimes I see fate's fingers
Scratch their nails on human hope.

Thoughts

My past lives in quiet reflection,
Filled with days of struggle and want,
Where sounds of need from foreign tongues
Attack Rabbis armored in black
Who pass naked hope about.
Mothers yearn for moments of stillness,
While fathers search for steady work.
Children race to play in the street
And long for a toy to keep them warm.
My mind recorded such segments of care
And life's regards are centered in there.

An Offer

If I sell my heart today
What value will it bring,
Filled with years of stress and love
And dregs from tested spring?

Calcite spikes scar its walls,
Worry robs its wealth;
Honor clears and warms its stream,
Terror steals its health.

A slave inside my earthly worth
All bidders shy away,
Except the soul who pays a price
Then lets it run and stay.

Paradise Enow

There's always peace in paradise –
Scheherazade unlimited –
Where happiness reigns status in quo
And produce and wealth deprive want.
Omniscience replaces all learning,
Families perch on a single tree,
And everyone dwells there forever.

A few beset with foreign disease
Babble of places of toil and hope
And chant in peculiar tones of prayer
Invoking fancies to be there.

Unnamed Graveyards

The running tombs along the tracks
Reach out like beggars with busted eyes,
And plants, tired from struggles to grow,
Produce only wild scraggy shoots.
Chunks of broken granite lie scattered
About the ground like unburied bones in ancient
Cemeteries. A few discernible letters melt
On the blackened red bricks surrounded by rusted
Chain-link fencing topped with metal
Scarves of rolled and noded thunderbolts.
Even the boys are grown and gone
And no one is left to stone the unbroken
Windows. The distance is yards away,
Yet the time spans generations of labor.
The breezes work the vacated lines.
There's no rhythmic clacking sound of the train
Just a soft cushioned floating movement.

Au Bon Pain

She sat across from me, an everyday
Girl, with her straw lingering in inches of orange
Juice while she entered items into a black
Book with a green pen in her left hand.
Slips of paper lay on the table before her.
Some were zigzag and needed pulling to be read.
Others were curved like small Roman arches.
She sucked in more juice then released the straw which now
Displayed her teeth marks and a frayed end.
Fearful of offending her privacy, I averted my eyes
For a moment; when I returned them, she
Vanished and her table seemed darker and clear of signs.
The chair appeared to need slight alignment.

The Woods

The woods are counterpart to me
Their shadows breathe my air.
The birds awake to welcome me,
The lilacs strike fanfare.

All creatures know my friendly state
And rest as I appear.
The brooks cast diamonds in the sun
So rainbows bend quite near.

The naked ladies perfume me
As violets couch my head.
Is this the place of fabled mark
Which shelters Eden's gate?

When Death First Came

When death first came to visit me
He left with empty hands:
My cells refused his stay and never
Gave a breath; my heart
And will escaped his grasp, my blood
Outraced his sunless pace.

And now on borrowed time, I ponder
Choices free to seek
The truth of being and forge my story
Whole, or follow still
My daily route with sunshine at my back
Until he comes in welcome
Guise and settles matters flat.

Apothegm
Besides laws and tales of mystic lore
What answers nature and god, what more?

The Power of Words

Apart from common diet words alone
Create an armor forged inside the heart
And etch belief upon the mind no laser
Beam or torture claim can scarce anneal.

Battles bend opponents, truth outwits
The tyrant, mothers watch their children peek
Around neglected clocks; people discard
Sackcloth and search about for valid graves.

The Tall Soldier

How happy the tall soldier who knows
The foe and sheds all other wars
To win the single cause; but then
The end complete, all dormant battles
Return and nature's choice prevails.

From the crying womb until the wooden
Lock of death purges all life,
We struggle within ourselves over
Duty and faith and contend with others
For daily sustenance and social honor.

I've Seen the Angels Gather Round

I've seen the angels gather round
To serve a fragile birth, and read
The thoughts of men inscribed on sheets
Of sun and rolls of dusty weeds.
I've felt the joys of ages tick
Within my catholic heart, and felt
The inner springs of life about
The ancient sins that burned my soul.

And now as shadows slowly hide
My crafted words that once unlocked
Italic type, I move in pictures
Of myself and strive to sort each day,
Though widowed houses beckon me
To enter them with selfless key.

Stamps

We carry stamps upon ourselves
To show all others our intent
Which they decode, assess and sort
And form opinions based on rite.

All dress and speech are common marks
To air our need to be a part
Of social traffic culled by want
And file a claim of conscious selfhood.

Related actions tell their worth
And measure mix with time and place
To set dramatic scales of class
Which peers expect to rate our ware.

No inside skin or persiflage
Can long indent acquired bents;
Most people fit a varied range,
A few do suffer unaneled.

A Creative Form

I wish all poems would write away
And cease to cruise my mind:
They importune my daily tasks
And harass other seeding thoughts.

I dread their pestered raids which flash
To trigger restless nights
Or threaten business taxing skills
Or vanquish phatic social rules.

Only pen, pad and time
Can purge these haunting maladies
And bring a moment's blank repose
Before another surge implodes.

In course each image alters its way
And concepts never mused emerge,
Until the final line records
A collected form of divine recipes.

A Form of Drama

After the picture show concludes
Its drama stills the active heart
Then stops the mind in wordless awe
And probes through cells to reach the soul.
The credits roll, the music fades,
The screen unveils its diaper face;
Emotions wrought remain intact
Until the exit door is crossed
And time injects a slow return
Then ushers forth routine redress.
The sum effect is never lost:
Its riches serve to honor life.

Here Is Enough

When life decides to leave
I do not long beyond its time
For realms replete with lavish goods
And showered joys unending.
Such outside hopes reveal despair
And abrogate the truth of being.
An alien dream's no substitute
For human love and service:
To overcome welfare strife
Asserts our inward dignity,
While hugs from an awkward child
Provides us with unbounded wealth.
Heaven lies in happiness new
And thoughts of things once done.
To rest in nature after life
Is God's unfettered decree;
Immortal joy all souls partake
Our spirits moving ahead.

Education

Education's not a school
For those who seek for coin;
Training is the proper term
With facts to take along.

Body engineers and keepers
Of the mind and soul are token
Takers better trained
Than those who peddle noise.

Politicians use sweet terms
To polish forth their roles.
What would Newman answer those
Who pervert ancient goals?

The count behind, the battle still,
Some wide apart with things and money
Substitute the riches missed
By backing arts with tainted honey.

A Visit Below

On day while seeking answers
I traveled down below
To a place some people know so well
Whose pseudonym is hell.

The atmosphere was bleak and rare
With sooty heat beyond despair,
And faces wore a blur of red
And raced about in ashy dread.

I met the devil there
In masquerading wear
He seemed a busy fitful naught
Whose business some religions brought.

He held my scroll of sins
Which guaranteed my stay with him.
I denied his claim and soul power
And he turned and fled in cold cower.

My sins were burned and I returned
Forever banished from that place.
From my visit I gratefully learned
That disbelief is a Godly grace.

A Place Inbetween

I wandered to a state today
That was neither here nor there:
It lay between two concepts
Just dangling in the air.

It was not fair or ugly
Just sort of nondescript;
Above were doves and honey
Below a burning crypt.

It seemed a giant lift
That was stuck between floors;
The top and bottom were sheer
But without escape doors.

One group had fluffy beards
And dress unique to see:
They moved about in bathroom towels
Each one defined B.C.

The other group wore more
Or less, tweed to fancy free;
They walked about with letters
That read a clear A.D.

The B.C.'s thought a lot
But never seemed to know;
The A.D.'s never thought
But always liked to crow.

I left anon, my boredom grew,
This painless place yet unsublime,
Where no one felt at home
Just people waiting there in time.

A Brief Reflection

When traffic flees and moments still,
The heart sometimes reverses flow,
And the mind rewinds life's running
Years and selects a mood ago
To relive now in quiet thought.

And in a flicker I see an early day
Where a boy the size of myself knocks
On my past to come play in the field
In the morning sun among the buttercups
And lambs and to hear the lilacs talk
And the butterflies kiss bashfully while
Circling in the delicate streaming rays.
And to race through the growth, his hand in mine.
Upsetting the grasshoppers and the wild birds,
Who fly high above the honey bees,
Then fall to the ground like a thunderous
Giant and search the earth for violets.
Or to rest by a calm Granby brook
And watch a trout, still and clear
In the water, as though locked in ice, await
A sudden coming of a skating skipper.
And to hide in the high hay among
The quiet flowers and hear the call
Of friends, whose faces now are melting,
Though their voices ring so clearly yet.
And from the branch of a twisted oak, survey
The horizon, secure and powerful above
The world, and proclaim peacefully the joy
Of being to the clouds and the birds and the deer
In the woods. And the truth of that confession echoes
Across the listening summertime of nature.

The breath from a current shadow dissipates
All scenes and blows them into a bank
Of memories to await another revival.
O may such reveries continue to cement
The unity of my life and tacitly rebuke
The wanton feebleness of time's theft.

Welcome Now the Morning Spring

Welcome now the morning spring,
The heir approaches her divine throne:
Snow relaxes and washes the way
While bees emerge and hover in swarms.
Dormant trees awake and dress,
Nature's people appear in spurts
And cautiously move then pause to look.
Straw carpets are dyed to green
As the sun kisses and warms the air.
The dead revive in altered form
Their garb fitted to happy release.
This silent procession forges life
And plants hope in earth's blood.
Nothing negotiates this awful reign.

A Body Dresses Flesh and Heat

A body dresses flesh and heat
To speak and lure an active seed
Which grows and fosters nature's need
For further life and aim complete.

As time creates Matisse's form
The flesh and mind reject a storm
And seek to cancel current frays,
Content to cherish former days.

Times Away

To flee from habit brings some joys
And sacred wounds that hide among
Our other thoughts and pass unmasked
Until the heart detects their sites
And makes their yield burn again.

A boy before a nervous girl
Exchange their happy smiles and names
And play for hours with friends in groups
Then move apart to kiss untaught
And leave along the foreign stir.

And wayward meetings built on sound
Believers hear and hold as truths
Are merely masked reclining tales
Whose transient start and false intent
Unleash a sorrow never meant.

Routine and space reduce the past,
And yesterday's life revives in gleams
Like views of distant streams whose flow
Now runs in curves of silver streaks,
Their bodies dark in the morning sun.

Death Is Like a Hungry Axe

Death is like a hungry axe
That feeds upon life's sap
And hews away until its core
Is eaten through and seeps no more.

The arid shell now topples down
And hides beneath the ancient ground
Where gnawing time then grinds the bones
So nothing likely can be found.

This residue uniquely blends
With nature's blooming recipe.
A sponsor sifts the magic mix
And spring recites another spree.

As God pursues His merry trade
His henchman waits and hones a blade.

Death

I've seen it brush against the sky
And weed an ocean bed,
And watched it plow across the past
And cloak the earth with dread.

It claims no age or gender bar
And time's an empty span;
Its power known but secret source
Resides in mythic man.

Once met the question hangs obscure
For nature sifts what's left,
And smoothes away the ancient rift
To hide the pilgrim's theft.

A Naught at Times

A naught at times pervades the whole
And holds all life in empty place,
Where needed self and running thoughts
Appear to mind as foolish acts.

External words are unheard noise
Like sounds from Sunday's funny sheet
That stay in print and flee unseen
When moving fingers turn a page.

Inertia grips the body weight
And collapses cells to powdered piles
Indifferent to the wind's caress or rain
That kneads the mass of chalky paste.

Away at bay from routine time,
Love pauses to dress itself
While hope catches its breath nearby
And the soul turns to examine its Xrays.

Reflections in a Mall

The misty morning flies from the orange sun
And the splattering stream calls in the distance beyond
The dewy grass and field of corn, closer
The water skates around the granite boulders
Then falls to glistening blisters that roll and burst
And flow into a smooth dark pool.
A canopy of elms shade the soft ferns
Above the rich brown earth that perfumes
The air where the silent trout play tag
In the still rainbow setting. Along the banks
Wild whiskered groups of cosmos raise
Their cups to the yellowjackets who drink their toast
Between sips of marigolds. On pussy willow
Lanyards the fossil dragonflies rest
Their burnt matchstick bodies and biplaned wings
And spy the shy butterflies kiss.

Only bits of remembered truth remain
In place, uneroded yet by forgetfulness, to reveal
The nature of being and shadow living time.

The Heart Rejects

The heart rejects all quality pleas
Until some crumbled trinkets prove
Forgotten truths that polish thoughts
And gently squeeze a spongy penance.

The mind abhors all selfish wrong
But justifies its presence, until our soul
In open court evaluates the evidence.
This noble judge straightens doubt,
Then levies terms to rectify the regimen.

No cold charts or balanced rules
Alone can settle private accounts.

My Soul Petitions

My soul petitions other realms for care
Outside its current state where human needs
Arise to blunt its creed and daily work
Confines its truth to routine comments diffused.

A conscious search can seek a place now lost
In mind to rent for time and rest itself
Along the slanting sun or silent sea,
Perhaps in still shadows of the quiet wind.

Another Day in Milk and Honey

The morning jolts into sudden being
And casts a Nordic gloom about the day
As the timid sun creeps along the rubble.
The stony ground is carpeted with metal and scarred
With the din and wasted hopes of medieval battles.
Not a single seed can penetrate its hardness.
Empty faces move in dark bodies,
Thin with fear yet set for routine action.
Sometimes a distant crack snaps the air
And people rush instinctively to the spot to gather
Pieces of flesh and to clean the mess thoroughly
Better than a swarm of active hungry predators.
When closer it's like Normandy without the smell.
The explosions further damage ancient foundations.
After the cries, the prayers, and the burials end,
Everyone proceeds to work again cautiously.
A quiet, safe night covers all sleep.

A Woman in Union Station

Sat on the varnished oak bench and leaned
Forward to shower personal concerns on her quiet
Listener. Her swollen face was bruised and oily
And resembled stills of tired and beaten boxers.
Her hands scooped the air then dashed it away,
While nods and bobs often punctuated her words.
Her voice resonated through the wood and struck the spines
Of those seated nearby like pellets from a shotgun.
All ears were torn by the tale of a mother's woe
Over her daughter's struggle for domestic tranquillity.
The listener beside her remained unmoved, a stolid
Mannequin perched in neat display clothes.
After expelling her store of mental wounds,
She hardened calm like the granite cathedral at Yale.

Stages

The cackles move so soft and warm
Like morning sounds in secret brooks
Then grow into gusts of current
That ripple loud in seltzer lines.
A sudden fracture alters tone,
Diverts the flow to private calm
Before a later noise unites
All circled starts in cold non sequiturs.

Our Daily Bread

She changes clothes so often time cannot
Record the lightly sprinkled colored gowns
That wear to solid prime then ease away
The textured gray and slip to silky black.

She hides behind a screen of clouds and mounds
Of crusty hue and dresses naked eyes
Askance before the sun on ancient road
Retrieves her robes and follows the silent wake.

Did Thomas sense beneath his hill the same
Repeated wave? Did Plato see between
His thoughts the sparkled marble moving there?
All treasures stay, our chance to keep escapes.

The Delicate Balance

From rhythmic shaking bones the liquid seed
Explodes and burns the womb with racing joy
And grows beyond a senseless plant into life
That glistens alone in dark and dreamy ashes.
The soldiers' bodies rock and dip at Normandy,
Slow and cautious along the oily beach,
Like spiders searching their wired webs for unseen
Prey now caught by chance in their passing homes.
As thoughts drain from drying shells left
Uncapped like molted blood in time's running
Sun, all children kneel and rise in the pace
And touch the truth that opens the human union.
Life's tensile strength reaches nature
And its isomers balance eons of changing crowds.

Extrapolations

I cannot leave my mind alone
And allow traditional wind tunnels
To measure and direct my logarithmic base.
Some thoughts instead escape all time
And reach beyond computed stars
(Which wallow about measured marks)
To plant symbolic culture here.
I've stopped my breath in the desert
And stood in stages to contact myself.
Often I've watered the morning moons
While walking my soul around the yard.
I see the swell of eternity in a blossom
And hear poets chase subtle agonies.
A swift strap to my head awakens me.

Perfect Unions

Half comes before the birth of anything
And return to that requires life's half.
Sometime after the initial ache the quest
Can be sought and a union eventually found.
Affliction must be experienced before relief.
Victory is sweeter to those in pain than to those
Who battled and won unharmed; Keats sought
A merger to soothe his raspy breath and bring
Peace to his action and thought. A wounded soldier's
Searching cry longs for death to stand
Still and for darkness to shed its fragrant light.
A balanced threshold between love and service
Equals zero and is the doorstep to our eternal nature.

A Wander

Sometimes it comes when time departs
And thought escapes to leisure space
And scissored strips of being hang
Unsewn on patches torn with wear.

Now portraits hide in false regard
And shadows storm the slivered sun;
Pollution fills the empty soul,
Old sins awake to blare again.

The matter spreads until routine
Returns to salve the daunted seams
And bury symbols dark past life
Between the threads of vital signs.

Aristotelian Acorns in Reverse

There's ceaseless music everywhere and phatic
Noise via TV. We have games with which
To see and explore inside ourselves and recipes
With tissued ingredients to create new life.

Everything is given here but want.
Researchers brought us into place and left
Us with diversions while they sought better Edens.

Some people still play with ancient sets
And punch WWW. God often.

A Search for Heaven

All work's a search for heaven beset
By human needs that hinder routes
Of progress with lanes of fettered dependence.
Some diminish clutter to brief chores
And chart their souls for truth, instilling
In others beacons of hallowed hope.
Along the way, some halt, reflect
And realize they've missed earlier signposts,
But cannot reroute past time
And suffer unduly their wayward choice.
Many blind to themselves end
In cul-de-sacs and revolve in barren
Efforts that quickly escape to hobbies.
Pavlov's bell mimics their search.

A Summary of Life

Life's an event of some matter and time,
Brought into being by joyful implant
And grown between space by a colonist's cord,
Then ripened awake through subsident canals.

Stretching marks now begin and move
Across a coil of defined rites,
As life passes through uneven oscillations,
Each action sustained by ticking blood.

Some aspects of sense are taken and stored
In volatile bits of unique files,
And often revived and seen within
Through mirrors shown on empty screens.

A persistent concept torments the mind:
The struggle to capture and understand death;
But obvious truth cannot be accepted
And foreign abstractions replace history.

A sudden sliver stops the heart
And eras of memory drain into stone.
The cycle of sign fades into symbol
Like granules of stars shattered in the night.

Dark Days

The sun no longer lights the days
But burns in silent dark
Among unfastened thoughts afloat
On ashes past decay.

The night has lost its hungry joy
And moves with neutral dreams
Among the scattered stars now dim
And singed from burning wear.

A shadow marks the melting snow
And evil turns all doors,
While time recaptures every hope
And wakes the soul's concern.

A Taste of Time

I live in a station where trains no longer stop,
Surrounded by fields as desolate now as they
Were when first discovered by happy seekers.
Time has erased the majesty of my being
And escorted the blank elsewhere to rewrite
Again the same words in fresher lines.
Old bricks wear well though and my house
Withstands the gnawing weather that relished little
The taste of colored clay; through opaque windows
I watch the passing faces and calculate the hope
In the eyes by the length of their smiles and their tears.
Such doings balance my side of the human equation
And help me to understand the patterns and simplicity of my creator,
And enable me to accept today with calm resolution.

A Hole in the Fence on Albany Avenue

It was hard to find in that red wooden fence,
Covered with ivy, sweetpea, and bristly foliage,
Which isolated the Queen Anne house from modern
Traffic and the prying interest of neighbors and passers-by.
But once the open knot was discovered, I sought
It each time I passed with wondrous anticipation
And peered through it into the view of the backyard.
A stone bird bath, a foreground of crab grass, and
A white trellised porch in vague shadows
Were all that could be perceived through the small hole;
Once I saw an old woman in a long draped skirt,
Which seemed to merge into the sunlight, move
Without steps toward the bath with watering can.
Yet, to see from the unseen held fascination for me,
As much as leering at a penny movie I cranked.

An Old Myth

Paradise was boring – it always stayed the same.
Rainbows showed their petticoats, Santa Claus
Unmasked, dreams were picked unheld by shame,
And wishes bathed each empty pause.

A candy store no better, a brothel focused keen,
An ear to capture chatter and food to sate the spleen.
Human want was lacking, pain in scarred retreat,
Goodness ruled incarnate and hope was in escheat.

I left the spot on hidden ground and came
Unto myself; once whole again by wrong,
I climbed my human cross and searched beyond
The perfect myth to where I could belong.

The Early Sun

The morning sun awakes the day
And fills the earth with light;
It visits homes and open space
And sweeps away the night.

With moving rays and buffing beams
It cleans the colored hills
Removes the clouds from yawning streams
And shines the daffodils.

The monarchs swim inside its realm
While spiders coil to sleep,
And bees retest their noisy wings
As frogs prepare to leap.

Initial chores complete, it warms
The shadowed seeds, then sheds
Its early clothes for silver mulch
And mints the fertile beds.

Whence the Coming?

Can private penance absolve public sins
That daily infect the sacred rights of humanity?
Do words early learned recited alone
Retain the force to adjust the world's imbalance?

Science is not equipped to track and calculate morality
That exists in wayward periods of altered continuity;
Will a forging Beowulf return from eternal myth
To quail unauthorized peril and wake the butterflies?

The Spirit's Prison

How can I flee this prison that locks
My spirit within and keeps it chained
To need while feathering its toil with pain?
The warden's way treats of things
Propounded by guards who rule his tongue.
My sentence unknown, a tick of the clock,
My crime accomplice to human sin,
A myth of ages the guards begin.
When time has ended and these walls have fallen
Away, will my spirits then be traded
And confined to linger in yet another cell?
Somehow my spirit and essence past all
Must transcend the source of enchanted relief
And reach a power higher than mortal belief.

I Tried My Hand

I tried my hand at acting
But its glamour didn't last,
Like guns and other playthings
I outgrew childish past.

I buried myself in music
And went along in school,
But practice and assignments
Became a harrowing gruel.

I wandered daily in the world
With time unmarked and thin.
The only things I cared about
Dealt with fun and sin.

Then one day it happened
I walked into a book,
Some words ignited up my back
And I had found my crook.

No matter where I say my prayers
Or how I earn my bread,
No other symbols transport me
With halos round my head.

It Isn't Fair to Die

It isn't fair to die and leave the day
Alone with fragile trace then further fade
Until the minds of those bereft do stray
To empty dark that time so quickly made.
The years that stood in struggled place at once
Forsook their war on life and spirit freed
Began the human epic learning acceptance
And tales of science wrought by magic seed.
How tragic now eternal loss this thing
More strong than spiked belief and tenured oak
That daily brought a common love to wring
Away the toil and fearful doubts uncloak.
The fireworks blaze each year in joyous sight
Then spread to taint and blacken quiet night.

Some Sins

Some sins the devil vacates based
On social change, though many last
   Without erase in older minds
   Beset by crusted lessons past.

   Morals built in holy time
Are often cracked by sheer neglect
And current temper weakens walls
   Of structures once upheld erect.

The law is fixed in fleeting rules,
   Religion creates conduct goals;
   A mix of blood confused thought
And human instincts tempt all souls.

Science strives to heal and grow,
   Unchained from daily belief;
Its symbols score untainted truth
   That cast mankind in relief.

A Spider Plots His Matrix

A spider plots his matrix while sun
   Unrolls its bed, each trajectory
   Is measured time to guide his lines
   And form an easel of symmetry.

An artist known by trademark his work
   Is hooked to air, it's seen by housewives
   Cleaning and children everywhere.
It can be passed unnoticed by persons unaware,
   But sudden fit of stop indicated it's there.

He waits outside his parlour door
   To greet a wayward guest,
   A tramp upon his complex route
   Is set with stirring zest.

One visit grows to final stay
   In private rooms of gauze,
   Accommodations tightly fit
   And built devoid of flaws.

The early light reveals his frame
   Now notched by nightly trade,
   Before he shakes his masterpiece
   And slowly draws its shade.

How Blessed I Trudge

How blessed I trudge this happy life
Within my sphere of time
And focus thoughts on garden guests
Through senses honed sublime.

The elephants above the sky with tongues
Of raspy gauze each day
Continue licking ancient rocks
And wear the hills away.

And bearded vultures feed on fat
From bones on lava mounds,
Where antelopes unchill their feet
And chase the genet sounds.

The dainty harlequins appear
A step ahead of spring
To model hints of colors keen
The earth intends to bring.

And winter covers cooling night
With jewels of icy stars,
While summer nectar warms each day
With juicy isobars.

All value alters changeless years
And fosters nature's ties;
My wild and silent friends demur
A chit to close my eyes.

A Facet of Water

At Cota de Caza the water percolated rampantly,
Then surfed over an ancient saucer and stretched
In silver streaks down to a wavy glistened base,
Where it splattered itself in giggling sounds and united
Into families of air nodes that bubbled away.
Years ago at Milan a fountain spoke
The same calm sounds in universal tones.
A pipe by the road near Highland Lake
Gushed spring water that dashed the ground
And carved running veins along the earth.
An oak trough in Hartford held the same
Water whose surface floated in rainbow streaks
Until horses buried their noses in the array and drank
With polite sounds that created concentric undulations.

The Ashes Grew

The ashes grew from fiery tongues
While distant teeth chewed the sky
And people warm in timeless pose
Toasted the search with unfilled goblets.

How high the glitter dusts the air,
How quick the sea drinks and mixes;
Even a seamless forged wrap
Cannot contain the active spillage.

Prayers mark each wayward fleck
And nature reads the tags;
God directs her active hands
To vary reconstitution.

Sometimes In a Quiet Pause

Sometimes in a quiet pause I hear
The cries of children over my shoulder
Whose words unknown and dim with wear
Still struggle with life along
Neglected dents that mar my mind.

And as I turn to interpret and close
I see only the traces of feet
Racing across fallen leaves,
Or outlined faces on unfaded walls
Where pictures once hung steadily,

Or ink spots on old blotting
Paper browning like cathedral rays.
Whither can I flee from such sounds
And thoughts of pervading failure that gnaw
The soul and body without hope and acceptance?

Shadows

No words can smell a fragrant rose
Or touch the thoughts of paint,
A movement dim to cracking sounds
The palate helps to taint.

The rising surge to sudden thrill
A camera films opaque;
And time can't hold its running
Brain or stop a bleeding stake.

So little passes here to now
No media can employ,
The lasting things we talk about
Are broken shades of joy.

A Dot with Wire Legs

A dot with wire legs resides
In spaces everywhere,
His home a complex pattern made
Of lines across the air.

More still than ancient statue worn,
More poised than cobra snake,
His patient mien awaits reward
From prey in breeze's wake.

An insect touch on cabled thread
Evokes an instant fight;
His fangs unseen but deadly rare,
Unique the creature's bite.

A frenzied flurry follows next
To tie the catch in gauze,
And once the cushioned mummy's done
His fluids drain through straws.

I shun this horrid trespasser,
This ash that stuns the heart,
Whose sudden going fosters fear
Of when again he'll start.

Life Is a Constant Drama

Life is a constant drama in episodic
Acts performed by changing
Casts who begin their inherited
Roles with every birth.

Each death repeats a lyric scene
With leading players near
Who summon stress and silent tears
To end the moving part.

The soul is an abstract director
Whose talents remain unseen;
His coaching permeates the plot
And unifies its immortality.

The March Begins with Human Joy

The march begins with human joy
Expressions proud and sacred
That fuse all souls to naked one
And bless the undertaking.

The hand of nature drives the way
And time controls the pace,
While death explores unseen detours
Aligned with waiting graves.

The trudge alone save guiding chance
Is strewn with aching noise,
And thoughts that end in running circles
About perhaps what shouldn't be.

A curled punch from gaming board
Is seen and usually discarded;
All quietness snaps back in place
And fades in shadowed pain.

Old Time's a Patent Devil

Old time's a patent devil who steals
Our lives in daily ways;
He dominates all work and play
And stamps our passing days.

More prevalent than any god
He's worshipped everywhere,
His symbols grace our walls and wrists
Consulted here and there.

His devastation grows in glass
And locks in faded prints,
Though children show no bent to him
Adults enforce his stints.

His place is always hurried speed,
The tyrant never stays,
His maxims teach engrossing gain
That everyone obeys.

His reign is surely ended
When death annuls his rule,
No need to mock less creatures
For their fixed solemnity.

Holidays

If holidays mean leisure
With naughts to cradle work,
Are deaths welcome pleasures
That halt the common gruel?

But mores rule such interludes
And curb our private strains;
Things all dressed and quiet words
Arouse dull escapades.

Crocheted eyes veil scenes
Creased with awkward clothes
And mark untouched catered food
That melts in the oozing sun.

Perhaps pass unanswered thoughts
That linger in the sifted air
Than forgo aching veins
Which cleanse pruned delays.

Silent Seeds

How soon the silent seeds of spring
    Absorb the climate's fare
And show their leafy bonnets soft
    Then wrestle round the air.

The months spread an apron green
    And synthesize the alchemy,
While life plays in bonded trust
    In periods of harmony.

But slowly dries the mustard seed
    And coldness tightens hems,
The pockets empty wherewithal
    And strings untie to stems.

The movement passes bleak to white
    Unseen the coda done,
An interval reflects the sights
    Of smiles behind the sun.

The Lightning Streaks

The lightning streaks in glowing shocks
That gild the air between the clouds,
And thunder grows in rifle blasts
Until the final sequence cracks
The earth with single sonic boom.

Like nervous fingers lines of rain
Rehearse their liquid tunes across
The tiers of shingled harps on roofs,
While others beat with muffled strokes
On concrete drums in fierce array.

The pockets snap in burning wood
And trigger chords of dotted codes.
A cat secure in calm retreat
Ignores the frenzied sounds abroad
Continues thoughts of lasting rest.

If Quiet Homes

If quiet homes for buildings razed
    Reflect the current time,
What chance is there that future claims
    Will mark today's decline?

The pulsing heads of pigeons roll,
    Their eyes emit research,
The sand in Texas chokes the air,
    And layers peel from birch.

With mathless route the ants proceed
    In alternating lines,
Their daily stretch of endless work
    Performed without designs.

Were all the papers, tests, and toil
    Some faithless human drill?
The rhythmic sounds of water drops
    Emerged then bubbled still.

The Massive Rocks

The massive rocks along the shore
With jagged backs and rugged shapes
Resemble prehistoric mammals
Embedded on earth in standing sets
Caught somehow by time and frozen
Into calm and stoic stillness.

In raucous tumults the ceaseless knocking
Waves like slashing picks of ice
Seek to dislodge the solid humps;
On shore fronds of waves like swelling
Snakes spewing nuts and bolts
Coil around their sides and kiss
At curves in rising smacks of suds.

Near shore the vying splashes diminish
Into surges of hissing foam
That shoot across crystals of sand
And leave in retreat an imprint of spikes;
Steadfast birds frail and aloof
Secure in motionless spots atop
The rolling flow probe for prey
Disappear and return to same locations.

Two spirits watch the spectacle
From seats above the embankment
And dangle their feet in relaxed sway
Like children bored with fishing.

What Choice Had I

What choice had I, what empty chance,
What part did genes employ?
Did early site, parental might
Determine life's deploy?

Was ever there a sheer recourse
To be unfettered me?
To move without ancestral nudge,
Is that a possibility?

I feel the tug of nature too
The richness borne from soil,
And creatures wild and tame
Are kin to daily toil.

Am I the sum of numbers past
A product made not free?
Do I deceive myself with lies
About reality?

Like those ago and after me
Such questions fill with faith,
And answers grow in beds of hope
With blooms that never die.

My Life Begins Each Waking Day

My life begins each waking day
And stays until my final thought
Unties its weight and fades to sleep
On showered peace so finely wrought.

The time between repeats all things
And routine charts the way;
Events that mark our sojourn here
Are chiseled dates of clay.

Before my birth a zero here
No pulse or fleshy noise
So death will lead me back to there
Where nature maintains poise.

No feeling harsh, no racing joy
The travel short and fast
When life departs on final breath
And joins eternal last.

A Little Late

A little late in spring but still
　　Early for summer's state,
The growing green revives the final
　　Ashes in winter's grate.

The signs so common sudden change
　　The symbols dress for time:
The empty church awakes to song
　　And warblers trill in rhyme.

The graveyard pictures smell a rose
　　And smile in louder peace
Which convicts view across the street
　　And mark their jail release.

Light dances in the mica walks
　　From granite stones to school,
Where teacher snaps her girdle loud
　　And eases golden rule.

The routine days of burned life
　　No longer hold and mound,
Candy is free in every store
And Indian pennies litter the ground.

How Little Life Expends

How little life expends to art
So much to chance and needs
That lock our thoughts in passing things
Renewed by daily creeds.

All values fade with desuetude
No preacher's talk sustain
The periodic exercise
Recalls our noble strain.

The business part of nature teems
With brutal intercourse,
And summer trees unbutton leaves
All change includes remorse.

Though running time does pillage life
Some items still are left:
Creative symbols strong and fast
Were overlooked in theft.

The Sun No Longer Sets Rewards

The sun no longer sets rewards
Or honors daily toil
Its former glories shadow light
On subjects grown disloyal.

The moon's an ancient souvenir
Of love debased to lust
That hangs its foreign effigy above
A worn and salty bust.

And time the scion lost by days
Repeats its empty rounds
Across the paper business aims
Now burnt in wasted sounds.

How soon the liquid amber turns
The spring again to whole;
How soon the tears of yesterday
Awake the dormant soul.

Another Spring

Another spring arrives this way
To focus optic cells,
Its lilacs measure fragrant scales,
Its crows check decibels.

The taste is cauterized with green
Of garden peppergrass,
While silky aments fill the dells,
And test the touch of class.

This yearly checkup free of charge
Includes a living drug,
Whose power eases body valves
And tunes the heart's old tug.

The potion also shocks the spine
And activates the mind;
A nature food that feeds the soul
And sheds the phoenix bind.

This holy treatment, vital fare,
No physician can induce,
Did ever quack practitioner
Such a miracle produce?

All Children Battle Healthy Sleep

All children battle healthy sleep
For fear of losing life
Because its prolonged empty span
Revives the natal strife.

This innate notion blends anew
In forms of insecurity;
Decisions open fearful thoughts
Alive with immaturity.

But when results are later weighed
All changes mark advance,
And wishes often race about
The want of sooner chance.

And nature eases altered states
With time to heart and mind;
No doubt should mar the final change
A turn of proper kind.

One Creature in Nature

One creature in nature I truly abhor
Resides in places out of the day,
But suddenly there by a shrub or a stream
A line appears that slithers away.

His tongue pulsates like thread uncurled,
And bitter eyes indict his mien;
If sound disturbs his naked pause,
He creates paths of wavy green.

Sometimes when turning a pasture rock
I set his offspring twisting in eights,
But fascination soon yields to fear
As sense apprehends nearby their mates.

If I should meet him one day vis-à-vis,
My mettle surely tested would be;
Would my body halt and my blood dissipate,
While time escaped with life but not me?

To lessen chance meetings before a swim
I bash the pond with stone or brick;
At night I whistle and walk with noise
Direct a torch above my stick.

A Mattress of Gossip

A mattress of gossip bores me to sleep,
And rusty noise elicits a groan;
Somewhere between dull intercourse
A set smile hardens to stone.

A pernicious din that drugs all thought
And lures my time astray
Resounds from a television box
Without its hypnotic ray.

The voices in books communicate
Without a tarnished sound,
Each printed word reveals a force –
Transports the mind around.

The prattle of children alive with nonsense
Are bewitching orators of state,
They turn reality to positive dreams
To which the heart can relate.

Update on an Urn

The children's smiles from dated faces caught
On glossy print evoke a warmth that floods
The heart and races about to heat a thought
That spills the eyes and runs in growing buds
Down sunken routes plowed by strokes of time.
A pause to notice now things before unseen:
The back of a walking stranger held in prime
Step about to enter the shadowed glean
Of buildings beyond the fingers of barren trees
Silhouetted on stones by winter's sun.
The flags on cars curl in the muffled breeze.
Everyone is quiet in this moment undone.
The crumbling record becomes a sacredness
That immortalizes life and awakens stillness.

She Came with Welcome Sound

She came with a welcome sound in the night
And guided my youthful stretch with ease
Of snow in a drying web of the eyes.

Her face was a phantom's line like a Greek
Composite of Eves unreal and ideal
Now new and imagined shape on the mind.

Her voice fell with notes that rippled through bars
Of heart and my blood unwaxed in its heat
Like calm undulations wrought by a breath.

Her body embraced my soul and her kiss
Undressed the furnace door of delight
That hypnotized me like glow from a coal.

Our confident love so little and young,
Alive with eternal thoughts uncompared,
Was ruptured one day by negative pride

And passed unconcerned through daily routine
Until the romance of time recomposed
The lost existence in sacred retreat.

Forever the forlorn vestiges ring
At night when the snow resounds off the lids
Of lamps and then dances round in the rays.

Nature's Atoms

When nature's atoms kiss the eyes
Symbolic hues and sizes flow
Through heart to fill and sort the mind,
The real reduced to measured time.

Some say the opposite is true,
That optics cast for stimuli
And store their glean in magic nets,
A sacred part of memory.

These ancient dares impinge our thoughts
And mix with new discoveries;
Each answer breeds another link
That tightens human symmetry.

But more than reason fills the soul
Which welcomes smiles of truth and beauty
And seeks a place when death importunes
Beyond the now and physical things.

Can Shakespeare hear his words tomorrow?
Do Handel's notes move him still?
Something else is left with the matter,
The immortal union does greatly please.

Life Is an Interlude

Life is an interlude of questions
Perhaps between two blanks,
Filled with talk and toil
And thoughts of perceived death.

Faith covers answers;
Some research the matter;
Acceptance of the movement
Brings us soft serenity.

Renewal acts the role of time.

O To Be Alive

O to be alive this day
And view its early rise,
And saunter free the waking fields
And nature's work apprize.

The sun invades night's privacy
And sets its easel there,
Then quickly tints the morning light
And orange pops the air.

The streams eschew their inky clothes
And change to clearer wear;
The flowers wake in decibels
To welcome bees with flair.

The crows assume a lacquered sheen
While monarchs sawtooth dance;
A puffy cat with peeking eyes
Observes beyond his glance.

This calm ascension trips the heart
And activates all states,
No task exceeds its time or fund
Acceptance regulates.

The Sun's an Old Physician

The sun's an old physician skilled
In terms of life support,
Whose practice covers living things
With wise and calm disport.

His frequent visits last all year,
Exams are done each day;
He moves about his patients pose
To check each cell and stay.

The scalpel, drugs and instruments
Are now the modern ways
To cure the foul ingredients
He burns with healing rays.

The plants absorb his sweetened balm,
His light implants a tree,
People daily take a dose
Of his vitamin D.

When done he leaves a colored treat
Of hope across the sky,
A thoughtful wave to soothe the mind
And feed the hungry eye.

Old Age Again

Old age is a wizened thief,
Who steals the tone from skin
And shrinks the eyes to almond stares
And weeds the hair too thin.

He sifts the bones with burning rakes
And cracks the marrow there,
Then excavates the warmth from cells
And taints the blood with care.

The mirror shows his shaping work
And lack of artistry;
The sagging lines and puffy orbs
Refute his sophistry.

No one can halt the pillage
Or stop his mentor time,
Or calculate the silent scars
That hide his inside crime.

The mind at times retapes old thoughts,
Ignores the robbing force,
But once upon review of things
Accepts the current course.

When Mirrors Move

When mirrors move in measured stops
    Across reflected years,
They take account of altered views
    Which time politely shears.

A photograph portrays detail
    Of microscopic pause,
A fleeting glimpse of running time
    Now caught like cells of gauze.

Today's disguise so sure and real
    Contests with former grace,
Immortal self reveals no truth
    And wears a changing face.

Emotions' Well

Emotions' well erupts in tears
That gush through springs of eyes
And taint the cheeks with wet debris,
Blunt manifestations of the heart.

Sometimes they sing like Christmas bells
With gentle sound of joy,
Whose meaning vis-à-vis the soul
Electrifies all life.

Sometimes they fall from gulping grief
That still all thought with pain
And soil the face with holy beads
No words or penance grace.

They later dry to sandy grains,
Erode by time and mind,
And fade away in silent flight
Like fireworks at night.

Race with Time

I care no more to race with time
To meet specific dates,
Where waking life defers to goals
That business calculates.

To barter wants and claim secure
Are priced with hidden cost,
Including stolen months and years
That calendar the loss.

So many blessings passed and viewed
From acting shadowed eyes;
All senses stolid, grown awry,
Unanchored wasted ties.

Allotted funds and words contrite
Cannot defray my debt;
A check or halt of target time
Will not redeem the mortgage.

She Left Us

She left us in the morning
On a slight and shifty day;
Goodbye was a moaning shiver
That bent then brushed away.

She took our love with her
And thoughts of who she was;
The stillness in the box was
A thing unknown to me.

Strange clothes and non-essentials
Her wardrobe didn't need;
Her scanty vestiges now dwell
On a sinking stone and a card.

I try often to think of her being,
But time gets in my way;
Sometimes a passing inkling
Wakes to scratch my heart.

Certain Moods

In certain moods we dwell on sins,
On haunting past transgressions,
That neither time can confiscate
Nor thought their warp amend.

Betray and flit of early love
Arouse a growing grief
That cankers still in heart's retreat
And beats a lifelong wear.

The stolen hope from young and pure
A thief-taker cannot replace;
The careless crack of human spirit
Spreads to lame the soul.

No words can cleanse nor acts repair
Afflictions' many kind;
Forgiveness keeps no antidote
For torments loose in mind.

No Fault with Crows

I find no fault with crows,
Their banter suits me fine;
And bees that enter wood
Are frequent friends of mine.

The minnows' silent talk each day
Confutes the sloshing stream,
And skippers quite above it all
Conjoin despite their sanctity.

A rabbit's steady eyes exude
A softness quite secure,
And warblers duel with hummingbirds
In lavatera's folds.

The antics of the butterflies who wrestle
With the air elicit cheers
From stately blooms whose coffers vie
To nourish them in pause.

How ripe this morning canticle,
This vineyard of the soul,
That leads me still in daily prayer
To comprehend the whole.

A Fearful Doubt

At times a fearful doubt intrudes
    Upon a mind between
The work of life and playful time
    With tears of pain unseen.

Its term a tight defining scar
    That rakes across the heart
And caps the breath in silent shock
    Then cracks the limbs apart.

All nature shuns its shackling force
    The naked ladies dress,
The quiet shadows hide the breeze,
    The sun exudes duress.

But when its burning grasp is most
    And seeks an utter scope,
The soul produces laughter's cure
    Restores exacted hope.

The Living Can't Abide

The living can't abide with death
  His here remains unseen
  Like closing elevator doors
  That cause a sudden screen.

His presence unpredictable,
He brooks no taste for time,
But comes about on any date
That suits his whim or clime.

Physicians know him very well,
  Though never introduced,
They hear his foreign tongue in speech
  From body sounds induced.

The king of democratic rules,
  He favors young and old,
And conquers any sex or race,
  The timid ones and bold.

Above the realm of human law
  He often flouts requests,
But acts in full symbolic now
When thought by God's behests.

Commentary with Poem

In Brentano's, apart from the noisy commercial prose
That hammers customers like flashy carnival barkers,
There are volumes of poetry in frail paperbacks jammed
Together on shelves like a crowded school of koi
Awaiting the keeper's esthetic net to free
Time from the murky imprisoned pond of unread words.

Only a few chart these isolated aisles.

Some who seek the refuge for warmth and shelter
Jar loose a random volume and flip
Through its pages in a chair, pausing occasionally
On a page to ride their thoughts over syllables,
Slowly intoning the words, then stopping to look
About hoping that no one will disturb their meager quiet.

Others dressed to fit a concept enter
The aisles and scan cantish poets while lounging
In striked poses; after a suitable perusal
They abandon the volumes and leave with happy thoughts
Of intellectual accomplishment frozen in their vapid blood.

In defense of their economic struggles some teachers in frayed
Dated clothes gather a few obscure volumes,
Not in school libraries, for potential journal articles
No one but peers will read and perhaps enjoy.
In line they ponder their ability to convince graduate
Students the significance of Browning's *The Ring and the Book*.

A balanced few, deliberate in their steps, the largest
Buyers of poetry, sift through the shelves quietly
And evaluate their responses to the volumes of magic words.
They walk the rows with slight sweet curves.
Their movement leaves a wake of silent exhalations.

The highest thoughts of noble things
And view of nature's soul
Are sacred gifts bestowed on those
Who ply the poet's role.

The magic song of being,
The pain of reaching not,
All lives between the endings
And those beyond the plot.
Are concepts wrought but still unborn,
Great visions felt inside,
A touching glow of heart and mind
Across time's dark divide.

But then the tragic version starts,
As symbols clash with signs.
When poets seek to echo truths
Expression hides in lines.

Their whittled words cannot create
A comet's dying run,
Or stab a whale with flaming pen
Unskilled to catch the sun.

Alone in Time

I left myself alone in time
And went to visit thought;
The journey wafted over dreams
And into answers sought.

The setting like a garden bloomed,
Equations grew in stalks,
Allusions filled each row with signs
And words aligned the walks.

My mind perused the boundless space,
All questions found their chemistry;
The final matter solved itself
In beds of rare geography.

Joy to Be Alive

What a joy to be alive today
And hug the morning sun,
And feel the quiet breeze awake
And start the daily run.

Within a rose a bee untwists
And cleans the night away;
The crows above accent the sound
Of mocking birds at play.

The colored flowers calm the mind
The heart invites each quest;
All nature smiles inside the soul
Away from time's unrest.

The simple life in Chaucer's day
Aroused his basic glee;
To Shakespeare's broader worldly scope
Such things a fool would see.

Splendor

On certain times a splendor comes
On fresh whispered mornings,
And spreads across the soft stillness
A quiet sense of eternity.

Foxgloves mute their dotted bells
Pictures cease to talk,
Hollyhocks open their periscopes,
And words retain no thoughts.

Years empty our struggling creeds
Before the awful presence,
Body and mind lose meaning,
The soul occludes its essence.

The Essence Lies

The essence lies behind something else
Which in turn leads to others and further
Trails like opening boxes within boxes
And then finally it's not even there.

It's like a reflection in a pool:
You put it there but it's not you;
Or take apart a foreign photograph
And analyze the shadow of a building.

Frances waters the earth and flowers grow;
She uses an ATM card,
Babysits, and watches TV.
She, instinctively, and Plato know it's not here.

Die in Pieces

We die in pieces not at once
As many fail to see,
A day's account is measured time
And filed in history.

The children rest in yellow peace,
Adults in routine red,
All bodies sag in cyclic waves
From weight of living dead.

Like night through quiet sleep,
The eras pass imperceptibly
And added life to life they sum
The ceaseless line of immortality.

Matter of Waiting

Life is a matter if waiting
From birth until our death
In the functions of commerce and playing
Along with age and breadth.

Clocks are symbolic durations
A way to measure stay;
Coefficients of time are equations
To while away delay.

Stoppage of time's the solution
To end the rule of pause,
Since eternity indicated moving
If there's no judgment clause.

Doubts are the things of forever
Another form of hold;
A celestial enclave must be found to
Unleash the spirit's mold.

A Hallway

Outside the open door I met
With time who scribbled notes and led
My start across a span of glitter
Into being which presaged my route and end.
Words lighted my passage and the ceiling
Waited for painted eyes to color
Its plaster, while wrinkled wallpaper from foreign
Smells measured my days in rites.
The floor was dented with shoemarks preserved
In wax like harried names on stone.
The linear route had few spikes
To otherwise shame my constant symmetry
Whose meaning hides behind senses.
And now as my muscles still wrestle
With pieces of time until they vanish
Into naked bones, my thoughts run
Like bleeding shadows which sing in the curved
Wind and fuel the rocking sea.

On Keats

His pen revealed prayers of serenity
Which longed for calm and peace away
From the throat-burning crystals and painful
Coughs which manifested his tortured cells.
The odes are a momentary flight from self,
An escape of spirit to wander with nature
Unbound by time and seek permanence
From transient life in the nervous rustling
Of Eugenia leaves and on designs of clay.
Life is a union of motion and absorption
Whose joy resides in art beyond time,
While art is the medium of transmission of life
From spirit to spirit in generational sequence
Like the bold infinity of facing mirrors.

Graduation in Nipomo

The people swarmed about the stands
And airhorns littered the patient air.
The mountains, beige and dry, had streaks
Of white across their faces, as if some hand had
Tried to excise them with a dirty eraser.

The students emerged in two straight lines,
Moving out of step to Elgar's march,
In billowy reddish gowns which hid
Their dress above the thongs and high heels.
Mortarboards slanted their heads awkwardly.

The program began: Speeches, then music,
Then further words of promise preceded
The name calling and tramp to the platform
Before the rite concluded with the parade
Of empty frames through the aisle of teachers.

The workman quickly cleared the field
Of the decorative five-gallon pots of junipers
And lavateras which rustled like skirts of showgirls
As they were hustled away. Footsteps echoed
Across the hollow platform, the microphone

Listened for voices, the empty chairs collapsed
To their knees and everything was set right again
As the wide night invaded the field.
In town, the quondam boys drank beer and jousted,
While the young ladies danced in ideal dreams.

Research

If I could cleanse the heart of care
How fast the stag would run.
If I could halt the wanton cells
What statues move so Greek.
If I could cure ill on ill
What prayers could I fulfill.
If I could bone a formless growth
Would angels awe my skill?
If I played life with loaded dice
Would God still ante up?

Contrast

One time no thought could step so far,
Though feet could peddle round the earth;
And hands by choice could stars unhook
And carry them to stretch each day.
Sense uncaptured probed all life
And trespassed bounds without reserve.

As reason swelled with daily rites
The past began to bloom in thought
Then slowly hide in milky sweet.
The window frame became the world
And shadows of leaves enlivened walls,
While nature's aches impugned belief
And time ticked to welcome change.

Acute Angles

Life's a ladder of ritual rungs
Set against a wall of time
Which nature nudges us to climb,
Common rungs at the factual ends
Measure life in terms of length,
While those between are rooted lore,
Mores fused with our personal states.
Numbers vary steps by choice
With chance a factor born unthought.
Sacred words cannot still or redeem
Rings of current moving us.
The final rung remains above
Denotation; each step resounds with cracks
Of weight like dice unseen against the wall.

A Barker

Pull the curtain; start the show;
Many people want to see
The start and growth inside the womb,
Where time unseen expands its work.

Get your tickets; very cheap;
Life's old wonder only felt
Before can now be seen in whole.
An ultrasound defies all doubt.

Hurry, Hurry, the miracle's here!!
Greatest story ever told
Is wrapped in living paper scans,
The surging stuff is caught on film.

Listen, brother, better come –
Google can't detect its source –
And turn off remote control TV,
And join the crowd in search of God.

Midnight Chow

Each grabbed a battered tray and greeted
Others in line and talked and laughed.
They watched the cook splatter eggs
Onto the greasy grill and spoon out cold
Spuds; hard toast and coffee were choices.

They ate in groups and told of humorous
Exploits, each contributing details to another's
Narrative; then they laughed alone and were quiet.
Some smoked while others embraced their coffee
Mugs. They rose in sync and laughed

Again as they slammed their trays empty
Against the insides of the garbage pails,
Placed them onto the revolving belt, and marched
Briskly into the night; their voices faded
As the screen door bounced behind them.

Cauldrons of fire from the afterburners blasted
The ground as the aircraft scrambled for interceptions.
Soon the night was quiet again
And only the exclamation marks of lightning
Bugs disturbed the holy dark.

The following night most returned and joked
Perfunctorily before each entered a reverie
And stared with empty eyes and thoughts
Into nothing while clutching their white mugs.
They rose on cue and entered the dark.

Long-winged roaches paused near the garbage
Pails, their brown bodies glistened
In the hazy light. Some then flitted
About the room, attempting to reach
The open piles of discarded food.

Lines

The clouds had smiling faces couched
Above a golden bed of happy
People filled with thoughts about
The coming ride and joys expected.

Although places differ and years
Fit into numbers, with varying degrees
Of pleasure or hope, the movement at Auschwitz
Or Disneyland remains the same.

Quarter-ton persons with backpacks
And rolls of flesh draped over their belts
Hobble in turn along with those with cramped
Belongings clutched in their skinny hands.

Barking uniforms direct progress
No matter where for the endless time
Of human dreams before life
Finally balances emotions to zero.

History

Outside of Greece, about a foot to the left,
There is enough dirt and stone to make
One wink and then fade away,
Imperceptibly.

CSULB: 50 Years Today

My throat burned from the cold morning breeze
As I crossed the sun and descended toward a sea
Of black with colored streams that crowded near trees
Around concrete holes, then shuffled on key
Bound for the Pyramid in awkward lines resembling
Images of old Jews swelling into railroad cars.
As I neared the busy talking cloudy walking
Teachers, I noticed their clay faces and scars
That reminded me of worn Halloween masks damp
With breath, and I listened to their phatic noise of time
The weather and ephemeral events with nothing of stamp
To mark the reverence I held for them in their prime.
My mind refused to melt the passing sight,
And kindle thoughts once sweet with sacred light.

The parade ended in the auditorium where the faculty fell
Into rackety chairs, then stared about with defunct eyes
From crowded coffins, while family and friends issued a yell
At them and waved wildly from the balcony to apprize
Them of their presence and seek recognition as though
These teachers suddenly appeared to public view
Like Roman soldiers returning from heroic woe.
A skit of 1949 in revue
Began and sounds from that long lost year
Stilled other thoughts with reflective balms
Until the talks of praise from names unclear
Destroyed the forlorn mood with progressive psalms.
Ideas preached of gain and social change
Were sterile concepts short of Newman's range.

After the service, queues formed for cheese,
Fried chicken, and Swedish meatballs; with plate
And drink in hand I carefully managed to squeeze

Into a chair at my quondam department and ate
While some in robes smiled and chatted politely,
Then paused to hear my queries about missing faculty;
But as each mouth repeated the names ever so lightly
I knew that brief time eroded their memory
Like the letters on weather-washed tombstones at the Granary.
And young ones between pauses could not recall
Other times with once green chemistry
That echoed the start of a never-ending hall.
I left in warmth and heard my steps unroll
Across the concrete air and grassy knoll.

Changes

Old man Winski has always been dead.
Annie Mather still gets water from
The well.   Little Josie now has a boyfriend,
And Hilary staggers over her feet.
The whole idea tickles the heart and mind.

Violinist on the Subway

A black morocco case, scuffed at the edges,
Lay on her lap, and her formal robe
And neck frill wrinkled in a shopping bag
Beside her. Some boys nearby laughed and
Nudged one another. An old woman
With a sack of clinking bottles complained
To her about her hapless life. She
Answered in monosyllables or short accented
Sentences. When quiet came she scanned
The ads above the handrails then closed
Her eyes and thought of the years of
Urgent practice in noisy flats and of
Her performance this night at Lincoln
Center. A smile powdered her face as
She sat in disguised clothes and swayed
With the subway's rhythm home to the Village.

A Butterfly

As sun unwraps the waiting shadows
And life in quiet whisper stirs,
Foxgloves raise their horns in praise
To welcome the sudden butterfly.
With indecisive moves and sightless
Train, it flits above constituents
Then stoops to kiss and chat with one
Before waving again in search
Of other groups and choices shy.
Like a sylphic poem translating the air,
The busy monarch pursues its hectic
Plan and coats blossoms with glory
Then departs with soundless nonchalance
And grants all things its majestic signature.

When Wolves Turn White Once More

Houses moved and sidewalks bent
And places known weren't there.
Patterns of rain reversed their flight
And noisy pulses crushed my ears.
The green leaves fell at sight
And slapped the coffin with empty hands.
Sounds inside recalled ago
And spots stilled my walking thoughts.
Images faded to a single name
And a face and scenes arose which gnawed
Aloud syllables racing backward.
Now alone in shrinking bones time
Narrows like puddled waters and stays
In sparks which fade in running shadows.

Homeless

Frightened of people yet begging,
He comes a sudden here, a hairy
Ape free within his own cage,
A mortal plight unleashed by fate,
Alone without social contract
Who hides and sleeps unscorned in cardboard
And bears unheard the pain of solitude.

Growing Shadows

They flee from me the happy days
When sunshine poured in rain
And greenness danced like kissing waves
Against my pleading will;
And nature roared in fond delight
While I performed in chant
The exercise of joy unbound
To years without recourse.
But now as Euclid's logic fades
My shadows touch the sun,
My fingers rest on former hands
Which tugged the spinning world,
And only slits of light remain
On courts where I had been.

To Hide a Thought

If I could choose a thought to hide
Beyond the wail of life,
Where silence captures busy noise
And calmness fills all ache,
I'd search my space of time's decree
And seek among events
For one whose meaning grasps the whole
And bury it with care.

Mindless Things

I'd like to purge my mind of things
Which occupy the barracks there
And come to life at random times
Undisciplined to work or ease.

Impressions made upon a boy
Explode like popcorn over flame
And mix with times under stress
Acquired during forgotten days.

No matter the years I've raked my mind
The loony tunes return and join
With awkward phrases to distort my thoughts
And linger alive like rhythmic prayers.

Some thoughts are spent with current ghosts,
Who clutter days and seal my wake,
While others space my taken years
And wait to mark my heart's repose.

Fast Food Outside

He sat on concrete steps and insisted that
His benefactor sit by him to absorb
His wisdom as payment for the rapid feast.
As he spoke his nibbled teeth chopped
The hamburger between sucks of coffee.
His eyes colored and his mind escaped
Its frame as he wandered to different spans
Of years while his bag of cans rolled
Away unattended in fits of wind.
Always bent forward from fear and
Cruel anticipation, he welcomed rest.
His steel wool beard grew into his
Oily hair and his face was so tarred
From the streets and weather that it was
Not possible to identify his former race.
He rose without thanks and leaned
Toward battle down the circled
Street with its haven of unknown goals.

After Shot

After shot a sudden sorrow grips
The heart with ice and burning pain
Which grows in hurt to wake and warn the soul.
The will suspends the common world and puts
Its sense in plastic still, as nature's laws
Arise to puzzle sweet symbols of life.
A changing pause regulates choice between
The empty zipper of eternity and the broken
Horror of reality. Whispered words convert
The mind and fingers pass over dogtags
To affirm human ties. Nearby two
Crows rattle the air. Then a setting in place
Starts and a wait in the ever-closing field.

Except in Thought

Except in thought too late to know the growth
Of children still in diapers, wailing needs
To parents who strive to learn their foreign tongues
And soothe all things corrupt in blankets of love.
No more the rhymes of Mother Goose who sleeps
In beds of books; no more the trucks in red
Alarming pages worn with words, and cows
With moos in letters cracked who talk to faded
Flowers below the sound of hovered birds.
And gone the frets which haunt the mind and char
The fringes of love. Before the hoping years
And prayers for success arrive, time will seal
The open years, yet can't repel the thrust
Of matter always swelling into life.

The Onyx Floor

The lights reflected twisted shapes which changed
Configurations on the black tiles as one
Altered one's line of sight across
The foot-square blocks, united by furrows
Of grout to form an impressive stillness beyond
The entryway a space and time apart.
A mirrored column caught the shoppers move
And held their images clearly before they passed
To the tiles which scanned their approach and streamed rapidly
Up legs to neutral crotches, back and hair.
Midway through the movements everything repeated
Then began to erase upward again
Until outside the area, half the diameter
Beyond the width of the tiles, all shoppers vanished
And the smooth blackness returned to quiet the floor
Except for a chance approach and the odd-shaped lights.

The Eyes Take Pictures

The eyes take pictures clear and sharp
And file those choice in mind's repose
Where future moments want review
To stir again the captive time.

A childhood land where heaven plays
Can flip behind action rites
Unseen by other camera clicks
And wanton curves which thresh the soul.

For years recall appears unchanged,
But dying cells dilute each frame
And awareness creeps slowly into
The fading dots of prints exposed.

No doctor's drug or magic song
Can halt each image's dimming march,
Though lingering passes may touch the mind
Or tease the heart with shadowed sparks.

Return to Change

Some houses moved while others bent
On streets where I once lived.
The empty lots where sunshine grew
Are filled with parking tar.

Foreign tongues which curled the air
And smells which danced delight
Have changed to hardened notes of slang
With hope erased in words.

Dylan

Begin again with twisting smiles and empty
    Shocks, while outside your time
I live nakedly, and talk to silent seconds,
    And question my blank heart, until a push
Cuts the clock and clasps our worlds together.

A wrinkled boy in blood and cream still
    Swinging after your bout with birth,
The horn in your belly blared the coming
    And your presence will warm man's
Sunshine, so rest with a humble welcome.

My other forever, a concrete knot of green
    And bone, take tomorrow's hand with all
The roots and fibers of yesterday's life swelling
    In your cells, and enter the growing love
That spans this heaven between eternities.

The Del

The uniformed clerks and attendants handled
The logistical functions with polite alacrity,
And the quests encountered in public places
Were holiday nice. A distant ship
On the horizon resembled a checkmark like the lines
Of a faraway seagull in a Cuprien painting.
The white wooden building stretched
Into a gigantic red rotunda, covered
By a tower balcony with an ornamental balustrade.
The massive structure overwhelmed the seascape
And, like a quiet living thing, watched
And pondered the plein air calmness of
Ancient San Diego Bay.
The women always settled matters
Of dining and entertainment with tact, unselfish
Thought, and concern for our common good.
Resentful of prolonged waits, persistent
Children found solace among
The sand-kissing waves whose hurried retreat
Left behind on the shore mystical
Treasures which beckoned to them in the sun.
Or with gleeful nonsense they played in the pool.
Until a later reading stilled
Their constant ticking and ushered them
Into peaceful night. In bed I felt
A warm glow issue from my wife
As she turned softly in her sleep.

There's No Evidence

There was a guy who had his lunch here
Each day for years; it was before your time.
We'd exchange polite comments and he'd
Unfold the comics and read them while he ate.
He'd turn to me sometimes and talk in sweet
Words about books and distant lands.
Once I noted his paper was marked with numbers,
Letters, and strange symbols. No one here
Remembers him, and I can't envision him now.
When a boy, I carved initials into a pine tree
Near the pond in Keaney Park in Hartford.
Some years later I noted new bark
Had erased or perhaps grew out of them.
I still see an old scar on my belly.

The March of Time

Caught by time in another day,
Sliced into dark and light hours,
Routine maps our starting point
And directs actions toward an end.

The hurry and go of some minutes
Are balanced by catches of breath,
And seconds of ponderous thought
Are idled by periods of rest.

No leader can halt its movement,
No power harness its flow,
Though life assembles its pieces
And marks their human account.

Children race in the sunshine careless
Of decree; matter blooms in a matrix,
A force sequence cannot impair.

Of All the Times

Of all the times that matter not
I'd choose the surplus age
Where past reflections float about
Like flotsam on lakes.

Of all the faults that manage me
Not one releases rest.
Demands require faithful pay
For being what I am.

The rule of action blanks all thought
As youth diverts in choice.
The years reveal what days ignore
In lessons savoir faire.

Like one and all I share the game
And fun on seats of hope.
My spell is set in cast roulette
With God inside the wheel.

Pro Life

I tried to turn my soul around
To gauge its sacred side,
But neither wine nor water disks
Could spell its human bond.

My practiced thoughts of rooted creeds
Demanded life through fear,
And sought to ease domestic need
With future grants for current faith.

One day when open clouds appeared
And sunshine washed all rain,
I felt a movement lift my soul
And turn in nature's place.
All shadows rose and time escaped
My training thought this truth;
Instead of reaching heaven by prayer
My soul already is living there.

After a Rain

Nature took a shower today
And washed herself clear and dark,
Then took a towel of sunbeams
To dry her clouds and peaky toes.

Wayward puddles found their homes
And the air breathed a fretless sigh;
The sky painted itself anew,
While the ocean stretched and set its curls.
Spiders admired their polished webs,
And the grass danced in spangled light.

How cute the outside smiled again
All dressed to walk in baby's bonnet.

Rain

The rain has no time to linger,
Its business can't cater delay;
It dashes along through the gutters
In furrows that swell its wide girth.
Bubbles and dots in the side shows
Race to the street to ride on its ribs,
While a thirsty monster, whose quencher is never
Appeased, waits at the end of the corner
To swallow the torrent through its grated mouth.
Plunging into loud darkness, the rain
Ruins itself and sunshine follows
In time to sweep aside its receipts.

Bumblebees

Like humming bomber aircraft the bumblebees
Cruise and hang heavily above
Potato vines and search the purple blossoms
For choice cuisine to feast upon.
Their ebon rounded forms, embossed with yellow
Streaks and trimmed with sharkish wings,
Are noted punctually as they glide into
Pockets of flowers, though some, upset
By foreign whimsy, peevishly figure skate
In swift procession about the air.
The stems all bow from mighty weight as gauzy
Scalpels operate with precise fury
To cleanse the pollen grains. The blossoms rejoice
With healthy snaps in place again
As the bees sweep away for further spoils.

At the Movies

It's not like in the new movies where a couple
Relaxes after sex and one smokes a cigarette
While the other reflects with a romantic smile
And they both gurgle happy, soft words
In a silky bed on a calm, wistful night.
It can be brutal and fierce in midday
Like a rape of a doubtful gorilla with forlorn
Thoughts about primitive days and sweet
Fruits and vines hanging in the humid air.
Or a lunchtime stop on hurried hour with a mother
Whose hands are tied to busy children rattling
Around the rooms whose walls warp with their sounds.
Or a young soldier, who, seconds later, runs
Away frightened and desires no further attachment.
Or a creative man who measures grunts and business,
Then politely retreats to his well-ordered world.
And the women don't lie there in smug content:
They have to clean themselves and balance this world,
And bear choices with ease and quiet grace.
Their hopes reside in life and their elusive ideals
Are the stuff old movies sometimes impart.

The Honeybees

Before the sun uncaps a yawn
The honeybees arrive
In opal dress with coded bars
The tissue pasted wings.
Like cough drops circling open mouths
They search the blooming beds
And pick a rose to seize upon
Then swoop into its core.
Their upturned bodies hail the air
As they loot the pollen grains
With gentle claws and hurried skills.
Refreshed the rose recoils,
Her random thieves partake their leave.

Return

The drive to visit places old,
Where once the thought of growth relieved
The daily want and prayers filled
Empty hope, lingers in mind
Now worn to velvet by lost time.
Rebuilt senses and voices mean
Are cherished as long forgotten days
Live again in welcome arms.
But secrets are held and the ideal quest
Mirrors no tales and the passing attempt
Moves in human dusk unknown.

Warblers

They come to breakfast early as sun
Completes its stretch and peck about
The sheltered vines where ants unwary
Tread. From one course to another
They flit and clean their plates and leap to
Other morsels of plentiful display.
Sated by empty stalks and cleanly
Shaven bark, they bounce upon
Loose wire to digest the ample meal,
Content to linger briefly they contemplate
A move and swing in varied rhythm
Then flash and bid the yard adieu.

All We Know

All we know is now and past
By words, pictures, sounds, and things.
They help us find ourselves in time
And serve to set matters of truth.
But means to future days reject
Our paltry funds except belief
Which uses thoughts to gamble reason
Whose odds so great an addict shuns.

If Perchance a Lustful Want

If perchance a lustful want, which swells
The hidden dome with time, should yield
To timeless chants of love and let
Delightful rockets soar inside
The dark and unknown way until,
Like dribbling wax, the passion ebbs,
Will mixed reactions follow then
With thoughts upon the torrid quest?
Doubts unsought may linger still
Before the current washes past
By wants anew which rule the mind,
As wild desire halts all growth.

A Short History Lesson

Our steps erode all marble stairs,
And statues corrode from carbon gas.
Names and other symbols change
With time and places cover themselves.
Wars intervene to hurry such matters
Past cycles of itches and bones.
Everyone loves to fix and create.

Valerie

Again the aches process the routine,
And tomorrow arrives from yesterday's life.
The moving miracle rubs abstract
Thoughts which charge the wisdom of bearded
Time and pulsate in a halo of love.

Another child born when the May air
Is sprinkled with the quiet fragrance of marigolds,
And butterflies are tickled by the morning sun.
O see the family senses light
From Valerie's heart-polishing movements.

As I reach to touch her jittery frame
My hand fades in hers and solidifies
Our mushroom flesh into a bone of immortality
That repels time's whittling persistence
And echoes life's space-sweeping joy.

ISBN 978-1-4675-8967-3